RUNS, HITS & ERRORS

Books by
JIM LANGFORD

The Game Is Never Over
The Cub Fan's Guide to Life
Runs, Hits & Errors
and
since 1983, the annual Cub Fan's Calendar

RUNS, HITS & ERRORS
A Treasury of
Cub History and Humor

Compiled by
JIM LANGFORD

Diamond Communications, Inc.
South Bend, Indiana

1987

RUNS, HITS & ERRORS
Copyright © 1987 by Diamond Communications, Inc.

Manufactured in the United States of America

DIAMOND COMMUNICATIONS, INC.
POST OFFICE BOX 88
SOUTH BEND, INDIANA 46624
(219) 287–5008

LIBRARY OF CONGRESS
Library of Congress Cataloging-in-Publication Data

Runs, hits & errors : a treasury of Cub history and humor / compiled
by Jim Langford.
    p. cm.
    Bibliography: p.
    ISBN 0–912083–22–0 : $14.95
    1. Chicago Cubs (Baseball team)—History. 2. Chicago Cubs
(Baseball team)—Anecdotes, facetiae, satire, etc. I. Langford,
Jim, 1937– . II. Title: Runs, hits, and errors.
GV875.C6R86 1987   87–27272
796.357′64′09773—dc19   CIP

For Grandma Guckien, Mary Pat and B.J.—
"It's in the genes."

CONTENTS

PREFACE

This book tells the story of the Chicago Cubs as players, managers, owners, sportswriters, columnists and fans have experienced it from the beginnings up to the present. The story is fascinating, at times dramatic and often funny, and the diversity of the voices that tell it in this book testifies to the love of the game—and particularly the Cubs—that has inspired this treasury of memories.

Here you will meet the magnates and managers, the stars and the unsung journeymen, the captains and characters who have created and sustained the Cubs for more than 11 decades. No one writer could tell the story as well as the contributors to this collection do. The variety of styles and slants makes this a trip through time with the Cubs as host.

I thank the following for their kindness and help in preparing *Runs, Hits & Errors*: Jill Langford, President and Publisher of Diamond Communications, for her patience, encouragement and cheerfulness; Ann Pouk of Diamond for her invaluable help in research and preparation of the manuscript; the *Chicago Tribune*; *Newsweek*; The Washington Post Writers Group; P.G. Putnam's Sons: William E. Geist; Bill Moor; Phoebe Medow; Ben Templeton and Tom Forman; and John Trever.

—Jim Langford
October 1987

—1—

BEGINNINGS

From the very day the National League was born in 1876, the Cubs were there, standing apart from other franchises with a manner and mystique all their own. In fact, the National League was founded by a Chicagoan precisely to insure that Chicago and the other western teams would no longer be subject to domination by the eastern teams in the National Association of Professional Baseball Players.

William A. Hulbert, who said that he would rather be a lamppost in Chicago than a big shot in any other city, was determined to bring a championship to the Windy City. In mid-season of 1875 he went to Boston to lure that team's leading pitcher, A. G. Spalding, into signing with Chicago for the next season. Not only did Hulbert get Spalding; Barnes, McVey, and White also decided to join Spalding in the move from Boston to Chicago. Next, Hulbert and Spalding convinced Adrian Anson to abandon Philadelphia for Chicago.

Eastern owners had been allowing contract jumping for years when it was in their favor and they were known as well to be soft on gambling and rules for the conduct of the game. Hulbert and Spalding knew that the owners of clubs in Boston, Philadelphia, New York, Brooklyn and Baltimore were certain to lower the boom on Chicago for daring to do what they themselves did all the time.

1

After meeting with officials of the other western teams such as Cincinnati, St. Louis and Louisville and gaining their support, Hulbert scheduled a meeting with the presidents of the eastern teams on February 2, 1876 at the Grand Central Hotel in New York. Using some good old-fashioned Chicago politics, Hulbert locked the door of the meeting room and held the owners captive while he spelled out his design for a new league. It worked and the National League was born with the expressed intent to curb gambling, contract abuses and rowdyism on the field and in the stands.

It is, of course, ironic that Chicago's entry in the new National League was named the White Stockings. Even so, the fact that "Stockings" is more classy than the name "Sox" used by the subsequent Chicago team in the American League 25 years later foreshadows the difference in tradition, style and fans of the two Chicago teams. Sort of like the difference between the executives of the *Chicago Tribune* and Eddie Einhorn.

It is well known that in 1876, the year in which General Custer made his last stand, Chicago won the first National League pennant. Led by Ross Barnes who hit .429 and manager-pitcher Spalding who went 47-13 with a 1.75 ERA, the Cubs (I refuse to call them White Stockings) tore through the competition with ease. Spalding played only one more year, and that as an infielder and not a pitcher, before turning the managerial reins over to Bob Ferguson for one year and then Cap Anson for the next 19 seasons

If there was a Mr. Cub of the 19th century, surely it was Anson. Though only an average fielder at first base, he was a splendid hitter who in 22 years with Chicago rapped 3,041 hits for a .334 lifetime average. As a manager he led his charges to five championships in his first

The Cub Champions of 1885.

eight tries and then went into a drought that lasted 11 years before he was fired after the 1897 season. The string of pennant-less years ran up to 20 before Frank Chance's Cubs took the flag in 1906. But by contemporary standards, 20 years is like a 30-minute rain delay compared to the current string of 42 and counting.

But back to the awesome Cubs of the '80s. The decade opened with three straight Cub championships. The 1880 Ansons won 67 and lost only 17, the highest winning ratio in baseball history. We know from the memoirs of A. G. Spalding that the Cubs of this period were a tough team in more ways than one. **Spalding recounts his efforts as president of the Cubs to curtail the wildest of his employees:**

The team was composed of fine ball players— there can be no doubt of that. It was playing winning ball right along, which made the administration of discipline all the more difficult. I knew that some of the men were drinking to excess; I was aware that these were keeping late hours; it was a notorious fact that their habits were altogether improper; but what reply could I make to their questions, "What's the matter with our game?" "Do you want us to win everything?" "Where's the team that can down us?"

One day I was remonstrating with Kelly, who was the liveliest of the bunch, when he turned on me with:

"What are you running here? A Sunday School or a Base Ball club?"

I told him that while we were not exactly in the Sunday School business we would still like to have the boys reasonably clean in their habits. The subject was dropped for a while and then I began to get letters from the public. Some were from prominent citizens and patrons of the game; others were from personal enemies of some of the players; still others were anonymous; but all told stories of drunkenness and debauchery, in which members of the White Stockings were implicated. These recounted scenes of revelry and carousing that were altogether reprehensible and disgusting. Finally the newspapers took it up and began to berate the management for the actions of the players.

Forbearance ceasing to be a virtue, I determined that something must be done; but what? As to myself, I could not charge the men with offenses I had not seen them commit. And yet I was reasonably certain of the existence of fire where there was so much smoke. I again interviewed Kelly and some of the others, telling them of rumors I had heard; but all denied the charges in toto—there was nothing to it, they insisted.

Meeting Billy Pinkerton one day, I mentioned my troubles and asked him to put a man on the job, with instructions to ascertain the facts and make a full report. In a few weeks the report was ready, and when I got it I did not know what to do with it. It was on foolscap sheets and bulked about an inch in thickness. It began with Anson, and dropped him after two or three days as all right. So with Sunday and several others. But the records of seven out of the fifteen players on the team were too awful for patient consideration. The detective had followed them up and down Clark Street, all over the tenderloin districts, through the whole roster of saloons and "speak-easy" resorts, and kept track of their

movements, in minutest detail, for days at a time—
and the evidence was now in my hands!

But what to do with it? That was a question not
easy to answer. If the full disciplinary powers of
the League were applied, that meant the disruption
of the team at the height of the season—the prac-
tical elimination of the White Stockings from the
League. I gave the subject long and careful consideration, and at length decided upon a course to
pursue.

One day I told Anson to have all the boys on the
grounds next morning, as I had something I wanted
to say to them. He asked me, "What's up?" and I told
him to be there and learn for himself.

Next morning I met the team by appointment.
I told them what had been done; how I had heard
the stories of their dissipation; how I had received
scores of letters of complaint; how newspapers had
finally taken up the subject; how I had then em-
ployed a detective to learn the facts, and that I had
his report with me. I then asked:

"Now, boys, what shall I do with it?"

"Read it," said one, and

"Read it," echoed the others.

I didn't propose to read that long grist again, and
so one of the players was deputized to perform the
task. He commenced with the report on Anson,
and I heard one of the players ejaculate, "Here's
where the old man gets off." A minute later someone whispered, "Here's where Billy (Sunday) slides
out," and so on until the real business of the report
began.

Unfeigned interest kept everyone silent until the
reading had ended. Then Kelly broke the silence

with one of his characteristic drolleries, saying: "I have to offer only one amendment. In that place where the detective reports me as taking a lemonade at 3 A.M. he's off. It was a straight whiskey; I never drank a lemonade at that hour in my life."

"Now, boys," I said, "what's to be done about it? I understand that you plead guilty to the indictment. What's to be the penalty?"

"That's up to you, sir."

"Anson, what's to be the punishment? Do you want to fine these men?"

"No," said Anson, "we don't want their money."

"I'll tell you what we will do," said I. "I appoint you seven men a committee to report the punishment to be inflicted upon yourselves."

"How much did you pay the detective?" asked one of the guilty.

"One hundred and seventy-five dollars," I replied.

"Well," said he, "there's just seven of us. Suppose we stand $25 apiece?"

"All right, I'm agreed," said one after the other, and thus ended the administration of discipline in that case.

As a sequel to this incident, another occurred a few days later. The White Stockings were about to leave for a series of games at Detroit. The train was ready to start. Standing on the platform was a great, green gawk of a fellow, staring with wide-mouthed interest at the departing players. Kelly caught sight of him and whispered something to McCormick. Then the "King" stepped up to the countryman and, after denouncing him in most violent terms as a Pinkerton detective, hauled off and smote him with all his might, while McCormick, coming up behind the bewildered "Rube," kicked the poor fellow's pants clear upon his shoulders. Then the bell rang and the belligerent ball players sprang to the platform of the rear car and went whirling Eastward.[1]

Mike "King" Kelly, a star of Chicago's pennant-winning teams of 1880, 1881, 1882, 1885 and 1886, recalled what being a winning Cub was like:

The lightest I ever played ball was 157 pounds with my uniform on. I had India rubber in my shoes then. I was like I was on springs, and I was playing with the best ball team ever put together—the Chicagos of 1882. I bar no team in the world when I say that. I know about the New York Giants, the Detroits and the Big Four, the 1886 St. Louis Browns and all of them, but they were never in it with the old 1882 gang that pulled down the pennant for Chicago. Then was when you saw ball playing, away up in the thirty-second degree. That was the crowd that showed the way to all the others. They towered over all ball teams like Salvator's record dwarfs all the other race horses. Where can you get a team with so many big men on its pay roll? There were seven of us six feet high, Anson, Goldsmith, Dalrymple, Gore, Williamson, Flint and myself being in that neighborhood. Larry Corcoran and Tommy Burns were the only small men on the team. Fred Pfeffer was then the greatest second baseman of them all. All you had to do was to throw anywhere near the bag, and he would get it—high, wide or on the ground. What a man he was to make a return throw; why, he could lay on his stomach and throw 100 yards then. Those old sports didn't know much about hitting the ball either; no, I guess they didn't. Only four of us had led the League in batting—Anson, Gore, Dalrymple and myself. We always wore the best uniforms that money could get, Spalding saw to that. We had big wide trousers, tight-fitting jerseys, with the arms cut out clear to the shoulder, and every man had on a different cap. We wore silk stockings. When we marched on a field with our big six-footers out in front it used to be a case of "eat 'em up, Jake." We had most of 'em whipped before we threw a ball. They were scared to death.[2]

Not all of the Cubs were dedicated to the high life. In 1886 in the midst of a close race between Chicago and Detroit for the National League Championship, Chicago outfielder Billy Sunday had what he described as a religious experience. **In the final meeting with Detroit with the outcome on the line, Sunday recalled:**

The last half of the ninth inning was being played. Two men were out and Detroit, with Charley Bennett at bat, had one man on second and another on third. He had two strikes on him and three balls called, when he fell on a ball with terrific force. It started for the clubhouse. Benches had been placed in the field for spectators and as I saw the ball sailing through my section of the air I realized that it was going over the crowd, and I called, "Get out of the way." The crowd opened and as I ran and leaped those benches I said one of the swiftest prayers that was ever offered. It was: "Lord, if you ever helped a mortal man, help me get that ball."

I went over the benches as though wings were carrying me up. I threw out my hand while in the air and the ball struck and stuck. The game was ours. Though the deduction is hardly orthodox, I am sure the Lord helped me catch that ball, and it was my first great lesson in prayer.

Al Johnson, brother of the present Mayor of Cleveland, ran up to me and handed me a ten dollar bill. "Buy a new hat, Bill," said he. "That catch won me $1,500."[3]

Sunday gave up baseball in 1890 and became evangelist Billy Sunday. It turned out that he was a better preacher than hitter anyway. His lifetime batting average in eight seasons was .248. **A news item dated July 20, 1911 from Erie, Pennsylvania noted his success:**

ERIE, Pa., July 20.—William A. Sunday, quondam professional Base Ball player, now professional revivalist, closed the evangelistic season of 1910–11 here the other day $70,507.77 to the good, as a result of his year's work "winning souls to Christ."

This return for about ten months' work, more than the President of the United States has drawn for the same time, is evidence that from a monetary standpoint, evangelistic work is more profitable than playing professional Base Ball. The Rev. Mr. Sunday recently refused an offer to go back to the "majors" once more. The inducement was but $500 a month. Seven thousand a month looks better to Billy. Besides he thinks he can do more good in the world preaching than playing ball!

During the past season Billy Sunday broke all evangelistic records for money earned. It brings the cost of Sunday's services to about $2 a "convert."[4]

Over the decades the Cubs have had many outfielders with lifetime averages of .248. Too bad they couldn't preach.

Even though Chicago could not beat their own won-lost record in 1881 and 1882, they won the pennant again both years. **Anson pinpointed what made his team tops for three straight years:**

The team that brought the pennant back to Chicago in the early '80s was a rattling good organization of ball players, as the "fans" who remember them can testify, and while they were the cracks of that time, and perhaps as strong a team as the League had seen up to that date, yet they were not as strong either as a team or as individual ball players as the team that represented Chicago several years afterward. The secret of the club's success in those days lay in its team work, and in the fact that a goodly portion of the time was spent in studying and developing the fine points of the game, which long practice made them fairly perfect in. There were one or two weak spots in its make-up, but so well did it perform as a whole that these weak spots were quite apt to be lost sight of when the time for summing up the result of the season's play had arrived.[5]

After finishing second in 1883 and fourth in 1884, Chicago got into a neck-and-neck race with New York for the flag in 1885. It is instructive for present-day Cub fans to know that the enmity between these two cities

Willie Hahn was the Cub mascot in 1883–85.

predates the 1969 outbreak by more than three-quarters of a century. The 1885 season came down to a four-game series between the two rivals, and New York needed to win three of them to take the pennant. Even though they were then the Giants and not the Mets, their genuine ancestry is verified by city rather than by logo.

New York fans came to Chicago in droves and in a betting mood. **Anson later recalled that even the newsmen who came with the Giants were caught up in the moment:**

There were a good many funny stories told about those closing games between New York and Chicago. The admirers of the Giants came on to witness the games in force, and so certain were they that their pets would win that they wagered their money on the result in the most reckless fashion.

Even the newspaper men who accompanied them on the trip caught the contagion. P. J. Donohue, of the *New York World*, since deceased, was one of the most reckless of these. He could see nothing in the race but New York, and no sooner had he struck the town than he began to hunt for someone who would take the Chicago end of the deal.

About nine o'clock the night before the playing of the first game he appeared in the *Inter Ocean* office and announced that he was looking for somebody who thought Chicago could win, as he wished to wager $100 on the result. He was accommodated by the sporting editor of that paper. The next night after the Giants had lost P. J. again appeared on the scene and announced his readiness to double up on the result of the second game. He was accommodated again, and again New York was the loser.

Still a third time did P. J. appear with an offer to double up the whole thing on the result of the next game. This looked like a bad bet for the local man, but local pride induced him to make the wager. For the third time the Giants went down before the White Stockings, and that night P. J. was missing, but a day or two afterwards he turned up quite crestfallen, and had a draft on New York cashed in order that he might get back home again.

Mr. Donohue was not the only man who went broke on the result, however. There was not a man on the delegation that accompanied the Giants that did not lose, and lose heavily on the games, which went a long ways toward illustrating the glorious uncertainties of base-ball.[6]

The 1886 Cubs repeated as champions but then lost a post-season series to St. Louis of the American Association, four games to two. St. Louis was managed by Charles A. Comiskey, who would later prove to be a thorn in the side of the Cubs on more than one occasion. Even so, Anson rated his '85 and '86 teams as the strongest he ever managed. But before the 1887 season, Mike Kelly's antics off the field led the Cubs to sell him to Boston for the small fortune of $10,000, and a year later the Cubs sent pitching ace John Clarkson to Boston for the same price. The Chicago papers did not take kindly to either transaction. The *Chicago News* went so far as to urge a reduction on ticket prices, claiming that if Chicago was going to have cheap players they ought to have cheap admission too. **Of Kelly, Anson later remembered:**

Mike Kelly, who afterwards became famous in baseball annals as the $10,000 beauty, came to Chicago from Cincinnati, and soon became a general favorite. He was a whole-souled, genial fellow, with a host of friends, and but one enemy, that one being himself.

Time and time again, I have heard him say that he would never be broke, and he died at just the right time to prevent such a contretemps from occurring. Money slipped through Mike's fingers as water slips through the meshes of a fisherman's net, and he was as fond of whisky as any representative of the Emerald Isle, but just the same he was a great ball player and one that became greater than he then was before ceasing to wear a Chicago uniform. He was as good a batter as anybody, and a great thrower, both from the catcher's position and from the field, more men being thrown out by him than by any other man that could be named. He was a good fielder when not bowled up, but when he was he sometimes failed to judge a fly ball correctly, though he would generally manage to get pretty close in under it. In such cases he would remark with a comical leer: "By Gad, I made it hit me gloves, anyhow."[7]

The loss of Kelly and Clarkson was compounded in 1889 when four stars and some lesser lights abandoned Chicago for the newly founded Player's League which challenged the National League by offering large salaries to contract jumpers. Anson was left with an inexperienced squad, "Anson's Colts," but he coached and coaxed his lads into a run at the pennant in 1891, losing out only in the final week of the season. From that point on things began to deteriorate. In 1892, Chicago came in seventh. Of the 1893 team Anson remembered:

It was a team of great promises and poor performances and no one could possibly have felt more disappointed than I did when the end of the season found us in ninth place, the lowest place the Chicago club had ever occupied in the pennant race since the formation of the League, we having won but 56 games while we had lost 71, a showing that was bad enough to bring tears to the eyes of an angel, let alone a team manager and captain.[8]

Then came eighth, fourth and fifth place finishes before Anson's final year, 1897. **His lament at the time has been echoed by later Cub managers, even some recent ones:**

The team with which I started out in 1897 was certainly good enough to win the pennant with, or at least to finish right up in the front rank, and that it failed to do either of these things can only be explained by the fact that underhanded work looking toward my downfall was indulged in by some of the players, who were aided and abetted by President Hart, he refusing to enforce the fines levied by myself as manager and in that way belittling my authority and making it impossible to enforce the discipline necessary to making the team a success. The ringleader in this business was Jimmy Ryan, between whom and the Club's President the most perfect understanding seemed to exist, and for this underhanded work Ryan was rewarded later by being made the team captain, a position that he was too unpopular with the players to hold, though it is generally thought he was allowed to draw the salary as per the agreement.[9]

Adrian "Cap" Anson, the Mr. Cub of the 19th century.

James A. Hart had succeeded Spalding as president
of the Cubs in 1891 and Spalding supported him in his
efforts to get rid of Anson. Sensing that the move was
unpopular, Spalding attempted to organize a testimonial to Anson with a goal of $50,000 in mind. But An-
son thought this would be like taking charity and he declined. "I refuse to accept anything in the shape of a gift.
The public owes me nothing. I am not old, I am not
weak and I am not a pauper," he said.

Cap tried his hand at running a bowling alley and
later a billiard room and he served two years as Chicago
city clerk but he wound up broke and with the mortgage
foreclosed on his home. He died in 1922 and a year later
a monument was erected to his memory at Oaklawn
Cemetery in Chicago.

**Of James Ryan, the player who led the dissent against
Anson, the *Chicago Journal* noted in 1898:**

I noted that a hit was wanted (for the Cubs) in
Louisville yesterday, and that James Ryan (who would
quit rather than play with Anson as manager) was
at the bat. How many, many times the cranks at the
Chicago ball grounds have waited and watched for
that same hit, and how often, oh, how often, they
have been regaled with that same play—a pop-up to
the infield. It is time, long, long ago, that James
Ryan was relegated to the bench or the turnstile—
for good. Decker is his superior in everything but
grumbling.

**What the *Chicago Tribune* wrote at the time of An-
son's dismissal could have been said as well at the end
of his life:**

For nearly thirty years Anson has stood among the foremost representatives of the national game, and for half that time he has been a popular hero whose name was more familiar on the lips of people than that of any statesman or soldier of his time . . . He possessed many of the qualities that make leaders of men, and his continued success was due to the same study and application which bring triumph in more highly esteemed fields of activity . . . Baseball owes him much, the public owes him something and Chicago owes him more.

−2−

DYNASTY

I t was only a year after the departure of one legend—
Anson—that another appeared on the scene. Frank
Chance showed up at spring training in 1898 to try out
as a catcher. "Anyone who at that time had predicted
that Chance was to become the leader of the greatest
club ever organized would have earned a laugh," recalled
Hugh Fullerton. Still, Chance made the team and endured with the other Cubs six seasons on a mediocre
baseball team. Manager Tom Burns had no more luck
than Anson before him and after two seasons he yielded
to Tom Loftus, who two years later gave way to Frank
Selee who helped the Cubs acquire all the elements of
a great team. He brought outfielder Jim Slagle from Baltimore, Joe Tinker from Portland, Johnny Evers from
Troy, New York, Mordecai Brown from St. Louis, Ed
Reulbach from Montpelier, Hofman from Des Moines
and Frank Schulte from Syracuse. And he moved Chance
from catcher to first. Initially, Chance refused to play
there and threatened to retire. Only a raise in salary was
enough to overcome his reluctance.

In mid-season of 1905, Manager Selee became sick
and had to resign. Some of the players didn't mind seeing him go. Selee was ready to get rid of Slagle and Evers
and he was so mad at Hofman that he refused to let
him practice with the team. The man selected to replace

Selee was the man called "Husk," "The Peerless Leader," Frank Chance. Johnny Evers records that the day Chance took over the team he said, "We need pitchers, a new third baseman and a hitting outfielder before we can win the pennant." A timeless call if there ever was one!

In the winter of 1905, James Hart sold the Cubs to C. Webb Murphy. Chance was given full power to run the club and he knew exactly who he wanted to complete his cast for the 1906 season: he got his third baseman in a trade for Harry Steinfeldt, his hitting outfielder in a trade for Jimmy Sheckard and his pitching in the purchase of Jack Pfeister and a trade for Orvie Overall. Thus strengthened, Chance's team swept through the League in 1906, breaking all records by winning 116 games and losing only 36. It had taken 20 years for the Cubs to win this pennant and they did so with such a vengeance that some observers thought it pointless even to hold a World Series that year. Especially since the American League banner was to be carried by the Chicago White Sox, the hitless wonders or runless hose who had eked out the pennant by a mere three games over New York.

The city of Chicago mobilized as never before or since for the occasion. **Johnny Evers remembered:**

Chicago is a Sunday ball town and the game on that day is the chief amusement of the people. And every town and hamlet, city, college, almost every church, young people's society and club, every farm hamlet and cross roads village has its baseball team.

The extent to which the people are familiar with the game and interested in it may be judged by a story. A few years ago the clubs representing Chicago in the American and National Leagues won the championships in their own leagues and met to

Cub fans celebrate a win in 1908 at West Side Park.
(Photo courtesy of the Chicago Historical Society)

play for the World's Championship. Chicago was in a turmoil for weeks, business was neglected, and work in many cases abandoned. The foreman of one of the great newspapers was compelled to send all the American League adherents in his office to one department and the National Leaguers to another, keeping them apart so the paper might be printed without delay. Police records showed hundreds of arrests of men who fought while disputing the merits of the two teams.

The Sunday editor of one paper sent three reporters out into the city to discover some adult male citizen who did not know that the White Sox and Cubs were to play. After five days of canvassing many sections of the city and all classes of its cosmopolitan population the man was found. He was a German butcher and he became famous in a day as the only man in Chicago who was ignorant of baseball and the approaching series. But even he became a convert, for Comiskey sent him a season ticket to the American League games and before the next June he was one of the regular White Sox rooters.

During that same series, when the West Side and the South Side were engaged almost in civil war, there was an Irishman named Faugh, a Ballagh Finnegan, better known as "Fog," who had made a small fortune in trade on the West Side, and who, although he never had seen a game, was one of the most loyal supporters of the West Side team. On the day of the first game "Fog," gloriously arrayed, and with much money to wager, was the center of a group of ardent West Siders assembled in one section of the South Side stands. Standing on his seat he defied the White Sox supporters and flaunted his money in their faces.

"Wan hundred to sixty on the Wist Side," he shouted.

"Wan hundrid to fifty. Wan hundrid to forty."

The South Siders, who were not betting on their team, ignored him. He shouted, challenged, and yelled the praises of the West Side. Presently the umpire brushed off the plate and announced:—

"Ladies and Gentlemen—The batteries for today's game will be Reulbach and Kling for the West Side. Walsh and Sullivan for the South Side."

For an instant "Fog" blinked hard, wavering between loyalty to the West Side and love of Ireland. Then, leaping up again, he shouted,

"Walsh and Sullivan—thim's they byes I meant. Wan hundred to sixty on the South Side."[1]

I cannot bring myself to recount in detail the way in which the White Sox won the Series in six games. Though it happened more than 80 years ago it is still the ultimate crusher in arguments between Cub and Sox fans; it is still the Cub fans' Mudville. **Let the following reprint from the *Chicago Tribune* say what needs to be said:**

Rev. Mr. Perkins (so-called because that isn't anything like his real name) is one of the shining lights of the Episcopalian Church in Chicago, a man noted for his high ideals and his good works.

Rev. Mr. Perkins has a son who strayed into strange ways, and finally wound up as a Base Ball reporter— and a corking good one. Indeed, he is almost as well known in his line as his reverend father is in his.

The son never laid any claim to being wise in his

father's line, but Rev. Mr. Perkins always has had quite an idea that he would have made quite as good a Base Ball reporter as minister.

Thereby hangs a tale. Last year the son was an ardent and faithful supporter of the Cubs. His heart was with Comiskey, but he couldn't see how Commy's bunch ever could beat Murphy's crew. His father, who attends Base Ball as often as there is no service, or meeting of the guild, was a wild and woolly admirer of the Sox, and one of the most ardent believers that they could beat anything on earth. And at home, instead of starting a discussion on higher criticism, the father and son debated strongly upon the relative merits of the South and West Side teams, and the debate waxed hotter and hotter as the post-season series came nearer.

Comiskey heard of it, and was so tickled that he sent the minister seats for all the post-season games—and it is stated that the church services during that week were adjusted to fit the post-season schedule—up to Sunday.

Rev. Mr. Perkins witnessed all the games, but on Sunday he was absent. It is stated that the afternoon services were cut short and that within a minute after pronouncing the benediction he was at a phone inquiring the score.

And that night he wrote to Comiskey a letter of congratulations, and at the close he said:

"It appears to me unfortunate both for myself and my church on this occasion that I was forbidden by my calling to wager upon the outcome. Otherwise I should have won enough to pay off the parish debt."

There was another fan who, on that memorable

Sunday afternoon when the Sox clinched their claim for the world's pennant, suffered. He is one of the best Base Ball cranks in Chicago, a rooter for the Sox and an ardent supporter of Comiskey. He has the good fortune (although he didn't think so that day) to have a good and pious wife, who is one of the leaders in a little church up in Edgewater. This fan isn't particularly religious, but he respects and admires his wife's stand in the matter, and during fifteen or twenty years of married life has assimilated more or less of her belief and feelings.

The post-season series, however, was too much for him. He attended five games and admits that he was planning to attend morning services with his wife and make a sneak to the ball park in the afternoon. Luck, however, was against him. A special afternoon service of great importance was announced, and his hope of seeing the deciding game evaporated. He knew he could not offer any excuse that would satisfy his wife, and that a plain explanation meant to hurt her feelings. So he decided to make a martyr of himself and attend the special service.

It is not believed that the service did him much good. His mind was away down on the Base Ball field.

He was sitting there, picturing the great throng on Commy's park, the excitement, the noise, the enthusiasm, and pulling hard for the Sox to win.

He wasn't even giving a thought to what was going on in church, and twice his wife had to pull his coattails to get him to stand up.

Suddenly he saw Deacon Morris arise and tiptoe into the vestry. He knew there was a telephone there, and for five minutes he had been wondering if he dared slip out and ask what the score was.

About five minutes later Deacon Morris tiptoed back up the aisle, smiling, and sat down just across the aisle.

The fan slipped along the pew, leaned out, and an instant later the worshipers in the surrounding pews heard him ask in a stage whisper:

"What's the score?"

And without a flicker of hesitation Deacon Morris whispered back, so he could be heard by half the church:

"Sox got 'em beat in the sixth."

For just an instant everybody looked startled, and then the minister, whether by accident or design, no one knows, remarked:

"Let us sing the long meter doxology."

But there is a minister out on the Northwest side who made himself one of the most popular men in the district on that same Sunday afternoon, when all Chicago and most of the world waited to hear the news.

There was a meeting of the Bible class called for 4.30 in the afternoon. This class is the biggest thing in the church, and almost all the men and women, especially the young ones, are members.

That Sunday afternoon the lecture room of the church was crowded—and the minister was late. He usually started things off, and then turned over the meeting to the class itself, explaining and helping only when needed or called upon. So the meeting was opened without him.

Shortly thereafter he came in, red from rapid walking, and beaming with smiles. He sat down until the hymn was finished, and then, walking forward, remarked:

"Ladies and Gentlemen: I have glorious news for

you. The White Sox are champions of the world—I
stopped to learn the score, feeling that we could
study better if we knew."

And the class broke into cheers.[2]

Having given the devil his due, there is nothing more to
be said about 1906.

The loss of four games was not about to deter Frank
Chance from achieving what he knew he was meant to
do. With the same lineup—Steinfeldt, Tinker, Evers and
Chance in the infield, Sheckard, Slagle and Schulte in
the outfield and Kling catching the likes of Brown, Reulbach, Pfeister and Lundgren—Chance led the Cubs to
the 1907 pennant.

Nothing could stop Chance's Cubs in 1907. With a record of 107-45 they swept the pennant by 17 games over
Pittsburgh. This time their opponent in the World Series
was the Detroit Tigers, led by Ty Cobb, Sam Crawford
and Wild Bill Donovan. Fate declared early that this was
the year of the Cubs. In game one, the Tigers were leading 3–1, in the bottom of the ninth. Chance led off with
a single and went to second as Steinfeldt was hit by a
pitch. Tinker popped up trying to bunt but Evers reached
on an error, filling the bases with one out. Chance scored
on a fielder's choice, making it 3–2 with two outs and
runners on second and third. The batter was Del Howard and he swung at and missed three straight curves.
But the Tiger catcher also missed the third strike and the
tying run scored on the passed ball. Mickey Owen, who
missed a third strike in the ninth inning of a Yankee–
Dodger game in 1941 should find some consolation in
knowing he's not the only one to have done that. In any
event, the game stayed tied until it was called at the end
of 12 on account of darkness.

The Peerless Leader, Frank Chance, whose Cub teams won 778
and lost only 396.
(Photo courtesy of the National Baseball Library, Cooperstown,
New York)

That tie was as close as the Tigers got to a win in the whole Series. The Cubs won, 3–1 and 5–1 in Chicago; 6–1 and 2–0 in Detroit. The Cubs won with pitching, (Cobb batted .200), baserunning (18 stolen bases), and what Johnny Evers called "the inside game"—the Cubs simply outthought, outmaneuvered and outplayed the opposition.

The year 1908 will likely always remain the most phenomenal in baseball history. Never before or since have the races in both leagues been so tight that one was decided on the last day of the season and the other in a one-game playoff.

When the World Champion Cubs gathered for spring training at Vicksburg, Mississippi, it was largely the same cast that had won two straight pennants and they had every reason to be confident. Almost from opening day on, it was a three-way battle between the Cubs, Giants and Pirates. These Cubs were just right for that kind of competition. Johnny Evers reports: "One of the Chicago pitchers, at the start of his career, was timid, and the batters kept encroaching on the plate and hitting his curve ball. Chance instructed the pitcher to hit one batter in the first inning of every game he pitched until the batters were driven back."[3]

The great sportswriter Grantland Rice later said of these Cubs:

There was never a ball club that loved a fight any better than the Cubs of Tinker and Evers and Chance. The Cubs of that day relished a fight so much that when they weren't fighting the enemy, they were fighting one another.

The story that Tinker and Evers didn't speak to

each other for a couple of years is well known. Less well known is the fact that Evers wasn't particularly friendly with some of the other players, especially Heinie Zimmerman, and that Tinker and Harry Steinfeldt, the third baseman, had many a wrangle and at least one fierce fight in the clubhouse.

With all that, however, the players were bound to each other by an intense loyalty to Husk—which was a name they had for Chance—and by their love for baseball. They were a hard-bitten crew.

Rice knew whereof he spoke. Witness the events of July 17, 1908, when Chicago and Mordecai Brown squared off against New York and Christy Mathewson. **W. A. Phalon of the *Chicago Journal* described what happened:**

The fans who came out yesterday grunting, disgruntled, sore, stung, and aching to vent their anger, went home pleased, flattered, satisfied and gleesome. They saw Brown pitch one of the greatest games of his career. They saw the Cubs, who had for a week played like Coshocton Gings on the back lots, round into fighting trim and put up a defense that was magnificent, and they saw Joseph Tinker.

Mr. Tinker was the whole works in several innings. It was his stop and throw to the plate that started a double play killing off the Giants with the bases full and runs sprouting like alfalfa in Pasadena. It was his superb pickup and hurl to first that beat Bridwell to the base by the eightieth of a step and saved another bundle of runs, and finally Joe delivered the goods with one of the grandest wallops ever scored on any field.

That romantic biff came in the fifth. Joe had two strikes called, and Matty was pitching a peculiar ball that came up with a high swing, then dropped suddenly and faded into the mitt of Rhino Bresnahan.

Joe aimed for the last of these, and got it. As the ball headed down deep left field, it was ticketed home run to a certainty, and the fans began to go insane.

As Joe turned third, artful Artie Devlin crossed his bows and delayed him some. He still had time and was keeping on, when H. Goat Zimmerman, coaching on the line, seized him and forced him back to third. Screams of rage rose from the people and the Cub bench. Joe took a look, saw that there still remained the slimmest sort of a chance, and shook H. Goat off furiously. He plunged for the plate and, Bridwell throwing with a strange slowness, beat the ball by the eighth of an inch.

The scene that followed was long to be remembered. People rose, smote one another, wailed, roared, guffawed and squalied. Tinker steamed on to the bench; Chance rose, and called in Zimmerman. What happened in the doghouse, screened by red awnings, no one knows, but the awnings shook as if mighty whales were battling in the deep and strange sounds of lurid dialogue, mingled with the batting of heads against the woodwork, streamed forth on the people, who rubbered hard but could not see. Whatever happened, H. Goat Zimmerman came forth to coach no more.[4]

In his magnificent book, *The Unforgettable Season*, G. H. Fleming reprints articles from New York papers dated July 18 and 24, 1908. No doubt about it, New York was gloating:

At a banquet in New York last December Johnny Evers declared that the absolute lack of friction between members of the Chicago team was responsible for its success, and that Frank Chance was like a father to the boys. Perhaps the lack of good feeling now keeps the Cubs out of first place. Perhaps Chance has become a stepfather. After a game lost this season Chance yelled at his men, "You're a fine lot of curs, you are." Not exactly the sort of talk boys expect from their father. Rumor has it that "curs" was not the word used, but it will do under the circumstances.

—New York Evening Mail

It is pretty well established that harmony does not exist in the ranks of the Chicago Cubs, at least not enough to call the champions a happy family. For some time rumors of dissension among the Cubs have been bandied about. Vague rumors have developed into reliable facts. The tale related here was told by two Chicago men close to the Chicago club, and verified by several players—not members of the New York club. Here are the alleged "inside" facts.

Just before the Cubs came East on their first trip it was announced that Sheckard's eyesight was nearly ruined by the explosion of a bottle of ammonia in the Chicago clubhouse. About the same time Zimmerman was sent to a hospital. Some excuse was made for his dropping out of the game so suddenly.

It has developed within the last few days that the injuries to Sheckard and Zimmerman were the result of a free-for-all fight in the Chicago clubhouse, in which Chance played a conspicuous part. According to our information, after a few hot words had been passed Zimmerman went at Sheckard. During the melee Sheckard threw something at Zimmerman.

Angered by this style of attack, Zimmerman picked up a bottle of ammonia and hurled it at Sheckard. The bottle struck Sheckard in the fore-head between the eyes. The force of the throw broke the bottle and the fluid streamed down Sheckard's face.

Manager Chance, thoroughly enraged, buckled into Zimmerman, and the uproar continued. Chance is known for his fighting prowess, but it is claimed that Zimmerman stood his ground until Chance called on other players for help. Then, it is alleged, Zimmerman was borne to the floor by force of su-perior numbers, and while he was down he received such a beating it was necessary to cart him to the hospital for repairs. Afterward the players took sides on the matter and the affair created bad feeling all around.

Sheckard and Zimmerman were out of the game for two or three weeks. That weakened the team, and when Schulte had to quit on account of illness the Cubs could not gain ground.

—*New York Globe*

In August when the Giants beat the Cubs and moved ahead of them by two-and-one-half games, the New York writers really had a field day:

When the Chicago Cubs won the National League pennant, a newspaperman out in Chicago started to call Frank Chance the "peerless leader." Today the Cubs are battling to keep their heads above fourth place and one does not hear much of the peerless leader thing unless a laugh goes with it.

—New York Evening Mail

W. F. Kirk of the *New York American* crowed:

We have it on good authority that Mr. Francois Chance gave an interview Saturday in which he alleged that the Giants had shot their bolt. "We have their number now," said Mr. Chance, "and they are due for a cleaning. They do not class with us." Right you are, Francois. They do not.

The haughty Cubs, as they lined up yesterday against the gingery Giants, were another Falstaff's army. They were so beaten up when the ninth inning was history they looked like so many Teddy bears in a second-hand store. Every time one of 'em got a wallop in the stomach he said "Ma-ma" just as cute.

New York pitcher George Wiltse said bluntly that the Cubs didn't have a chance:

Frank Chance's braves are not possessed of the proper spirit, in my estimation. Everything was lovely while the Windy City lads were showing a stern chase to the rest of the company. But when collared the Cubs have proved quite docile.

Apparently Wiltse couldn't collar the Cubs in his next start against them, opening a three-game series in Chicago on August 27. Jack the "Giant Killer" Pfeister beat Wiltse, 5–1. Chicago fans sensed their Cubs were ready.

Next Brown beat Masterson, 3–2. Not only was West Side Park crammed with fans, but 10,000 more fans jammed downtown Chicago to witness the *Chicago Tribune's* reproduction of the game using lights on a board to represent the players. Once as Brown was about to pitch, a streetcar blocked the view of those across the street from the game board, and people shouted, "Hold the ball a minute, Brownie, hold it."

Not done yet, the Cubs behind Jack the Giant Killer finished the three-game sweep with a 2 to 1 win. Now the Cubs entered September only one-half game behind New York.

On September 4 the Cubs lost a 10-inning game to the Pirates, 1–0. But the significance of that game only became clear later. With the bases loaded and two outs in the 10th, the Pirate batter sent a shot past Evers, apparently ending the game. Evers, however, called to Slagle for the ball and stepped on second because the Pirate runner from first hadn't even bothered to go to second, reasoning that the runner from third would score and the game was over. Unfortunately, Umpire Hank O'Day had also beat a hasty path to the exit when the hit went past Evers so he did not see the play and refused to listen to Evers' protest.

As G. H. Fleming uncovered in his research for *The Unforgettable Season,* on July 19 a letter was printed in the *Chicago Tribune* from a fan asking whether in such a circumstance the run counted. The answer was, of course, no. It is likely the Cubs, who were home at the time, read that letter and decided to be alert should the situation present itself.

By mid-September, New York had a lead of one-and-one-half games over Chicago and two over Pittsburgh. Things were definitely getting tense. Chance made Artie

Hofman postpone his marriage "for the good of the team." Hofman agreed because, he said, his bride-to-be "is as anxious to have the Cubs win as I am."

On September 22, the Cubs won two from the Giants in the Polo Grounds and pulled to within a game of the lead. Brown was the winner in both games, prompting a New York writer to comment: "It was not their fault the Giants lost. The team was overcome by 'Three-Finger' Brown, who finished the first game for Overall and pitched the whole second game. The only thing for Mc-Graw to do to beat Chicago is to dig up a pitcher with only two fingers."

Then, on September 23, came the celebrated game. The Giants had runners on first and third in the bottom of the ninth and the score tied, 1–1. Al Bridwell lined a hit to center and the runner came home from third with what seemed to be the winning run. Fred Merkle, the runner on first, did what many players did in those days—he didn't bother to go to second but headed for the clubhouse to evade the fans who were pouring out onto the field. Evers called for the ball, got Umpire Hank O'Day's attention, touched second and nullified the Giants' run. A near riot ensued, protests and counter-protests were lodged with the League and a week later President Pulliam declared the game a tie and declared that since neither club had an open date, the game would not be replayed. How was he to know that Chicago and New York would end the season tied for first with records of 98–55, one-half game ahead of Pittsburgh?

The game had to be replayed and the Cubs headed East for the showdown at the Polo Grounds. It is esti-mated that more than 250,000 people surged in and around the Polo Grounds on October 8. The attention of the whole country was focused on that diamond. Back

in Chicago everything stopped save for the sound of the
telegraph bringing in the description of the game. The
coroner of Chicago predicted despair, insanity and sui-
cides if the Cubs lost.

The Cubs in hostile territory showed their character.
Johnny Evers recalled:

> New York had the game won until the third inning
> in which Tinker was Chicago's first batter. During
> the entire season Tinker had been hitting Mathew-
> son hard, and the psychologic effect of past perfor-
> mances has much to do with pitching and batting.
> Mathewson feared Tinker and he signaled Seymour
> to play deep in center field. He was afraid that a
> long drive by Tinker might turn the tide of battle.
> Seymour saw the signal, but disregarded it, having
> an idea that Tinker would hit a low line fly, so he
> crept a few steps closer to the infield, instead of
> moving back. Matty dropped his famous "fade away"
> over the plate, and Tinker drove a long, high, line
> fly to left center. Seymour made a desperate effort
> to reach the ball, but fell a few feet short, and the
> ball rolled to the crowd in the outfield for a three-
> base hit and started a rally that gave Chicago the
> victory.[5]

Evers noted another key play of the game: The Giants
had two men on and Bresnahan was preparing to bunt:

> Kling caught the bunt signal, the ball was pitched
> out and like a flash Kling hurled the ball to Chance.
> Herzog was caught hesitating eight feet from the
> bag and New York was stopped in the midst of a
> rally that ought to have netted half a dozen runs.[6]

C. Webb Murphy, president of the Cubs, had predicted: "We will play them Thursday and we'll lick 'em too. We'll make it so decisive that no bone-headed baserunning can cast a shadow of doubt on the contest."

The Cubs made good on the president's claim, 4–2. **I. E. Sanborn of the *Chicago Tribune* said it all:**

NEW YORK, Oct. 8.—All honor will be given the Cubs as long as baseball is played, for what they did this afternoon in the shadow of Coogan's Bluff. They won not only decisively but cleanly and gamely, while their adversaries attempted to take cheap and tricky advantage of them in every way. The world's champions were compelled even to fight for the privilege of getting the meager practice allowed by the rules before the game.

Nor was defeat and loss of the pennant New York's only disgrace, for the crowd contained at least one man who will be remembered to Gotham's discredit as long as Merkle. That is the dastard who sneaked up behind Manager Chance as the Cubs were leaving the scene of victory and struck him a blow in the neck.

Before the Cub manager could wheel to defend himself the coward had been swallowed up in the tremendous throng. A hurried examination of the manager at the dressing room by a surgeon in attendance disclosed that the assailant probably had broken a cartilage in Chance's neck but it was not expected that the injury would keep him out of the world's series battles.[7]

The Cubs had no time to bask in their victory; they had to board a train for Detroit and a World Series rematch with the Tigers who, though they claimed the American League pennant on the last day of the season, had several days to rest and prepare for the Cubs.

The Cubs won the opener, 10–6, and the Series switched to Chicago where Wild Bill Donovan and Orvie Overall dueled in game two. A disputed homer by Tinker led the Cubs to a 6–1 win. **Evers recalled how Chance had set the strategy:**

Before the game meetings of both teams were held. Chance planned his campaign depending entirely upon which pitcher Detroit used, and his orders, issued the moment "Wild Bill" Donovan was selected, were conveyed to his men in one word: "Wait." They waited—waited—waited, while the huge crowd went wild as inning after inning reeled away and neither side was able to score a run. Donovan in that game had perhaps as much speed as any human being ever possessed. His fast ball jumped and darted and his curve, pitched with tremendous power and speed, broke almost at right angles.

Inning after inning as Chance sent his men to face that human gatling gun which was firing the National cannon ball at and around them, he monotonously commanded: "Wait," and they went up— and waited. One strike, one ball, two strikes, a foul, two balls, foul, foul, sometimes three strikes, sometimes a weak fly that netted nothing. To the crowd it seemed as if Donovan never could be beaten, as the champions appeared helpless before his tremendous speed. Still Chance commanded: "Wait— wait him out." Every batter went to the plate intent upon making Donovan pitch as many balls as possible. They fouled, they waited, sometimes even let him strike them out, sometimes they hit, but never until they were compelled to do so. When the eighth inning came neither had scored. Hofman led off that inning and still his orders were to wait, and he waited until he could wait no longer, then rolled a safe scratch hit down towards third. In that moment Chance, commanding general, ordered the charge. Tinker was the next batter and the order for the assault was the single word: "Switch." That was all, but Tinker, rushing eagerly forward to the batter's position, knew that the leash that had held the champions had been cut and that he could hit when he pleased, even the first ball. Crash, Tinker smoke the sphere a terrific blow and like a swallow the ball darted out to right field, high, higher, until, soaring far over the heads of the crowd it struck the sign above the right field seats and the crowd went wild. Then, like soldiers attacking a breached wall, the champions rushed to the assault and, before the inning was over, they had made six runs and their waiting game had won.[8]

The Tigers won the third game, 8–3, but Brown and Overall then pitched successive shutouts, 3–0 and 2–0, and once again the Cubs were champions of the world.

These tough and cagey Cubs played well again in 1909, winning 104 times while losing only 49. Unfortunately, the Pirates won 110 games and the pennant. But in 1910, Chance's boys were back on top by 13 games over New York. This time the World Series opponent was the Philadelphia A's, managed by Connie Mack, and the result left no doubt that the Cub dynasty was coming to an

end. The A's won easily, four games to one, and in the
process demolished the once great Cub pitching staff.

Decline set in, slowly at first and then more rapidly.
In 1911 the Cubs finished second to the Giants and a
year later, they came in third despite Heinie Zimmerman's Triple Crown season. The bitterness that attended
Cap Anson's dismissal in 1897 again showed up in Chicago as Chance and owner Murphy went public with
their mutual dislike.

As Warren Brown tells it:

Throughout his playing career, Chance had the
unhappy faculty of getting himself hit on the head
with pitched balls. He suffered great pains as a result of this, and eventually it was decided to oper-
ate on him for a supposed blood clot.

It was while he was hospitalized that owner Murphy came through with a statement denouncing the
Cubs as strayers from the straight and narrow path
of training. Among other things, he said that the
Cubs of 1913 would have to get along without their
rum ration.

Chance arose from his bed of pain and denounced
Murphy for this, while defending his players as normally sober and industrious, if not always of championship stature or even of major-league compe-
tency. But it was not until the formal parting of
the ways had come that Chance really reached the
heights in blistering statements about Murphy.

He characterized the club owner as one who
would not spend money for ballplayers or for the
improvement of the ball park. He maintained that
Murphy would not send scouts to the Class AA's or
to the Class A's but into leagues of lower classifica-

tion, so that any eventual purchases would cost but little.

"No manager can be a success without competent players," stormed Chance, "and some of these I have are anything but skilled. In all the time I have been with this club I have had to fight to get the players I wanted. Murphy has not spent one third as much for players as have other magnates. How can he expect to win championships without ballplayers?"

Again Chance maintained that he had argued with Murphy that other owners were paying out money, and that Murphy had replied: "If they want to be suckers and pay it, they can, but I won't."[9]

And so ended the Chance era. The Peerless Leader had led the Cubs to victory 753 times and suffered only 379 losses in the process. He was 21–11 in World Series play. He batted .297 in 15 years as a Cub and still holds the season and career stolen base records for a Cub. Chicago has never seen his equal.

— 3 —

STARTING OVER

With the departure of Frank Chance, the breakup of the Cubs went into high gear. Joe Tinker, Three Finger Brown, and Ed Reulbach were soon dispatched and although Johnny Evers was installed as manager of the Cubs, he lasted only for the 1913 season and then owner Murphy was set to trade him. Evers threatened to jump to the Federal League and that was more than the National League could take. A meeting was scheduled in February 1914 and Charles Taft of Cincinnati bought Murphy's 53 percent share of the Cubs. Things settled down. Evers went to Boston and helped them win the 1914 pennant. Meanwhile the new manager of the Cubs was Hank O'Day, the former umpire who had ruled against "Bonehead" Merkle back in 1908. Hank lasted one season before he was called out in favor of catcher Roger Bresnahan, who finished fourth in 1915.

Tinker came back to Chicago in 1914 to manage the Chicago Whales in the outlaw Federal League. He was joined a year later by Three-Finger Brown, whose 17–8 record helped the Whales win the pennant. Whales' owner Charles Weeghman survived the failure of the Federal League that year, bought the Cubs from Charles Taft, and moved them into his ball park at Clark and Addison. Although Weeghman installed Tinker as Cub manager, alas, he finished fifth and that finished him.

He was succeeded by Fred Mitchell, who lasted four whole seasons.

One of them, 1918, was a pretty good season, given the fact that the country went to war. The season was halted right after Labor Day, but permission was granted for a World Series to be held. Too bad. The Cubs squared off against the Boston Red Sox, led by a pitcher-outfielder named Babe Ruth. Worse than that, the Cubs decided to play the Chicago home games in Comiskey Park in the hope of attracting larger crowds than they could accommodate at Cubs Park. But the crowds didn't come—either in Chicago or Boston.

About the most exciting thing that happened in the Series was an angry, solo invasion of the Cub dugout by Red Sox coach Heinie Wagner, who didn't like the names he was being called. Ruth bested Hippo Vaughn, 1–0, in the opener; the Cubs won the next day, 3–1, but Boston took the third game, 2–1, before the Series moved to Boston, where Ruth won, 3–2. At that point the players went on strike in protest of the small shares they would be receiving, this being the first year that 30 percent of the receipts went to members of the second, third and fourth place teams.

"Honey Fitz" Fitzgerald, mayor of Boston and grandfather of John F. Kennedy, made a speech from home plate in Fenway, saying the game would be played for the sake of the wounded soldiers who were in the stands. The Cubs, behind Vaughn again, won 3–0. But the next day the Red Sox ended the Series with a 2–1 verdict and the Cubs were once again victims rather than victors.

Whether it was punishment for hosting the Series at Comiskey Park or because Babe Ruth scared them as much with his arm as his bat, or for some other and unknown reason, the fact is that the Cubs went into hibernation for 11 years before they won another chance at becoming World Champions.

Shortly after the World Series of 1918, William Wrigley, Jr. acquired enough stock to become majority owner of the Cubs. Foreshadowing later innovations by a Wrigley regarding Cub management, he named field manager Fred Mitchell to be both manager and president of the Cubs. The National League ruled that this was not a permissible combination and directed Wrigley to find another president or another manager. Whereupon Wrigley appointed as president a sportswriter who had been critical of the Cubs and who had answered Wrigley's question, "Could you do any better?" with a simple "I certainly couldn't do any worse." His name was William L. Veeck.

After finishing third in 1919, the year the White Sox nearly cost the game of baseball its life, and fifth the following year, Fred Mitchell probably wished he had been made president rather than manager. He gave way to Johnny Evers in 1921 who in turn yielded to Bill Killefer for the last third of the season on the way to a seventh-place finish. The next three years saw Killefer's Cubs check in fifth, fourth and fifth again, setting the stage for their first-ever visit to the basement, in 1925. Three managers—Killefer, Maranville and Gibson—nursed the Cubs through the season. Admittedly three managers in one year is not the same as a college of coaches, but it's close enough and the results were strikingly similar. Wrigley and Veeck were embarrassed and they went in search for a new manager and new players for 1926.

The following edited account of the revival of the Cubs under Joe McCarthy is excerpted from Warren Brown's *The Chicago Cubs:*

In his seven years as a Cub executive, as well as in his baseball-writing days for the *Chicago Evening American* before that, Bill Veeck's acquaintance with ballplayers in major leagues and in minors was perhaps as large as anyone's. From one and all who had ever played for, or had any dealings with, Joe McCarthy, Veeck had been unable to run across one who didn't have a boost for the Louisville manager.

They were agreed that he knew baseball and that he knew men and how to handle them. No one put a rap on him, which, in a sport which seems to thrive on second guessing, must have amazed Veeck, the seeker after information. McCarthy had never been a major-league ballplayer. The Class AA as an infielder had been the extent of his climbing before his playing career was ended and he turned to managing.

It was taking a long chance then to bring up this comparative unknown to big league ways, and give him custody of a ball club that wanted a championship more than it wanted anything else. Yet that was what Bill Veeck did. Thus entered into the Cubs' life a manager who will be ranked with the greatest of all time, though it must be admitted much of the McCarthy managerial record was made at New York and in the American League— but the Cubs must be scored an assist on the play. He didn't remain the Cubs' manager more than five years, but as he said himself, from his loftier eminence as a collector of American League and world championships for the New York Yankees:

"That was about par for the course. Since 1900 only Chance stayed any longer than I did. Anyhow it worked out all right in the long run for all of us, didn't it?"

To McCarthy was handed the material left over from a club that had finished a hilarious last in the 1925 sea-

son. He welcomed the opportunity, not on the negative
side that anything he did at all must be an improvement,
but with positive confidence that he could make good
with the resources of Wrigley and the backing of Veeck.

There were those on the ball club who had other ideas
about the new manager. Long inured to haphazard management and overcome by their own sense of major-
league importance, these players regarded McCarthy as
a "busher," and they had to be shown. He was not long
in showing them.

The ranking figure on the ball club was Grover Cleveland Alexander. In the 1919 season his 1.72 earned run
average set a Cub pitching record that has never been
equaled. Jim Vaughn's 1.74 the year before coming near-
est to it. In the 1920 season Alex turned in a 1.91 earned
run average. He led the Cub pitchers in seven successive
seasons. Old Pete had been a great pitcher—and would
be a great pitcher again, when he found the time.

It was one of baseball's tragedies that Alex had his
own peculiar ideas on keeping in condition. McCarthy
was not a hard taskmaster. He had been a ballplayer himself; he knew ballplayers. He knew that there were many
skilled performers who had their moments when they
batted against or pitched with John Barleycorn. He didn't
care so much, one way or another, about that. All he
asked was that his ballplayers be ready when game time
came, so that they might give him the best they had
when he asked for it.

Old Pete wasn't quite up to that a good part of the
time. Several times McCarthy called on him and Old
Pete wasn't ready. McCarthy had to make a quick judgment. He realized that Alexander, on his past pitching
record, was one of the game's greatest heroes, and that
getting rid of him by a "busher" in his first major-league

Cub hero, Hack Wilson, with his wife and child amid the admiring throng.

managerial season might well bring down the wrath of
Cub fandom. But to let Old Pete get away with it must
of necessity lead to the question: Has this manager any
guts? McCarthy had.

On June 22, 1926, Alexander was sold to St. Louis at
the waiver price. All baseball knew then that McCarthy
was managing the Cubs in fact as well as in name. There
was no resentment shown by either the departing great
pitcher or the remaining manager. Indeed, McCarthy
likes to tell yarns to this day of his experience with
Alexander.

One of these developed when McCarthy and his players met, as was their custom, to discuss ways and means
of pitching to hitters of an opposing club with which a
series was about to begin. One of the Cubs' misfits had
been dealt to this club a short time before, and the point
was raised whether it might not be advisable to change
the Cubs' signals.

While the discussion was at its height, Old Pete, who
had arrived late and promptly seemed to go to sleep in
a chair, made neither sound nor gesture.

"We've got to change our battery signs," insisted one
of the Cubs. "When So-and-so gets on second he'll be
able to call every pitch."

There was a slight stir in Old Pete's corner.

"If he was *ever* going to get on second base, McCarthy
wouldn't have let him go," said Alex—and took no further part in the meeting.

McCarthy's knowledge of American Association business, and especially its baseball standards, helped him
in his building up of the Cubs. At Toledo in 1925, playing
outfield, was the roly-poly, good-natured "Hack" Wilson.
He had been planted there by the New York Giants, who

for some reason had forgotten about him. McCarthy hadn't, and when the Cubs went to camp in 1926, Hack Wilson was a member of the cast.

Before he was to leave the club, which was soon after McCarthy did, this little round man was to hang up a National League home-run record which still stands, and a runs-batted-in record which all the batsmen of all time, National or American Leaguers, have been unable to equal.

Wilson was a high ball hitter on the field—and off it—but there wasn't a day in all the time McCarthy managed him that Hack wouldn't be on the job, ready to take his cuts when the baseball bell rang. He was in one scrape after another, but McCarthy forgave them all, because Wilson, for all his extracurricular activities, did give service on the ball field.

In one of the spring training junkets to California, the Cubs were playing exhibitions in Los Angeles. Hack got out of bounds one Saturday night, and McCarthy knew about it. The Cubs' manager was not one to maintain a house-detective system in running his ball club, and it could have been an accident that he found out about Wilson's being A.W.O.L. on this particular occasion. McCarthy happened to be on his way to church early Sunday morning when he saw Wilson zooming down the street in a car full of very, very jolly good fellows.

It was the custom for the Cubs, still in the training process, to go through lengthy batting and fielding drills before each exhibition game. Wilson, looking like anything but the well-trained athlete, was among the early arrivals at the park. He went promptly to work, keeping as far away from McCarthy as he could.

When the game began Hack was at his post in center

field. He was fairly dripping with perspiration, the day being unseasonably hot, and sweating it out was one of the best things Wilson did.

First time up Hack hit a home run that started the Cubs off on a rally. They kept on collecting runs until by the time the game was half over they had so many McCarthy mercifully removed his regulars—all but one—and sent in rookies. Wilson stayed in. Meanwhile he had hit his second home run. He was almost in a state of collapse now, but McCarthy gave no sign that anything was out of the ordinary.

In the seventh inning Hack teed off and hit one of the longest home runs that had ever been witnessed in the vicinity of Los Angeles. He was barely able to jog around the bases. When he returned to the dugout, McCarthy looked him over.

"Maybe you better go in now, Hack," he said, "or you'll be too tired to go riding again tonight."

Out of the American Association for McCarthy's first year with the Cubs came Riggs Stephenson, the "Old Hoss." He had served a four-year term in the American League with Cleveland before dropping back to the Association. There McCarthy recognized his hitting possibilities, and up came the Old Hoss to take his place in the Cub outfield.

The pitching staff also gained potential strength before the 1926 season opened. Charley Root, who had been out in the Pacific Coast League on option, was recalled. Pat Malone, who had been knocking around the minor leagues for several seasons, eventually landed with Minneapolis, and while toiling for that club, caught McCarthy's eye. Root and Malone joined up with such regulars as Percy Jones and "Sheriff" Blake.

Guy Bush had been recalled by the Cubs for 1925, but he had not yet acquired major-league polish. He wasn't as fearful of the big city as scout Jack Doyle, who found him in the deep south, says he was when first glimpsed. Doyle insists that Bush, upon learning that he had been sold to Chicago, hid out on several posses Doyle, the "Old Oriole," had sent to find him.

Nor was Bush as yet the glass of fashion and the mold of form he was to become when, as a most successful pitcher for the Cubs, he was to dress and look like something out of the "Sheik of Araby," or at very least, a Rudolph Valentino B picture. All that came later.

The Cubs might have had another outfielder for that 1926 season if McCarthy hadn't decided that his judgment of a ball player was better than that of William Wrigley, Jr., who just owned the ball club. During 1925 while sojourning in California, Wrigley had become attached to Frank "Lefty" O'Doul, a splendid-hitting outfielder who was then with the Salt Lake club.

O'Doul, a native San Franciscan and one of the foremost salesmen of the "Native Son" formula, had come up to the Yankees in 1919 as a pitcher. The Native Son formula, in case you have forgotten, calls for a refusal to admit at all times and in all other places that there could be any sector of the land comparable with California. If you come from San Francisco, as O'Doul did, that's the greatest place on earth. If you come from Los Angeles, that's the greatest place on earth. There is a song, "I Love You, California," you know—and it's the Native Son's National Anthem. O'Doul remained for two seasons, featured chiefly by his being the life of the many parties which Babe Ruth organized. O'Doul was returned to San Francisco without having added anything to the

Yankees' playing strength or having detracted therefrom. He was back in 1922 and then moved on to Boston, the Red Sox sending him out to Salt Lake in 1924.

O'Doul thrived on Coast League pitching. And Wrigley thought so well of him he one day asked Bill Lane, the Salt Lake owner, how much he wanted for the outfielder. Lane thought $15,000 would be about right, and Wrigley said it was a deal.

O'Doul showed up at camp with the Cubs at Catalina in the spring of 1926 but fouled out as far as McCarthy was concerned and was sent to Hollywood. Wrigley said not a word—then.

Later on, when O'Doul broke back into the National League, and either led it in hitting or caused damage to some Cub pitching hopes, Wrigley would sigh:

"Oh, that O'Doul . . . my O'Doul!"

Even though the Cubs made the 1926 race with no O'Doul, they were able to get back into the first division. Hack Wilson led the league's home-run hitters with twenty-one, equaling the mark set by Frank Schulte fifteen years before. Hack also led in drawing bases on balls, getting sixty-nine, every one of which made him more irritated than the one which went before. For Hack dearly loved to swing a bat at anything which came within swinging range. It didn't make any difference to him who pitched, or how. Hack was in there taking his cuts, supremely confident that one of them would land.

A particular source of annoyance to the Cub hitters was Dazzy Vance of the Dodgers, who had fanned seven of them in a row in 1924. Daz, who affected an undershirt whose right sleeve was torn and flapped while he went through his pitching motion, specialized in striking out Cubs. But Wilson never conceded Daz anything.

As soon as the Dodgers would come on the field on the days Vance was due to pitch, Hack, from across the field, would start hurling insults at the Dodger pitcher.

On the Cub squad as a utility player was the slightly built Clyde Beck. He once confided that Vance, in pitching to him, should be made to throw from second base.

One day at Wrigley Field, Vance was scheduled to work for the Dodgers, and Beck was to be in the Cubs' line-up. Just before the Dodgers came out for their warm-up, Wilson was in the Cubs' dugout rehearsing some new stuff to call Vance. Beck pleaded with him to keep the peace that day.

"I've got to hit against him," he protested, "and I don't want him stirred up any more than he usually is."

"Nuts," said Wilson. "The big bum can't break a pane of glass, and I can't wait to tell him so."

The Cubs were at batting practice when the Dodgers came out. Vance had just appeared when Hack let him have it, a complete new routine of sweet sentiment. Beck had been waiting his turn to take batting practice. But no more. He walked quietly back to the dugout and placed his bat under the bench.

"This isn't going to do me any good today," he said.

For the 1927 running, McCarthy reached into the American Association for another ballplayer to add to his cast. That was shortstop Elwood "Woody" English, who came up from Toledo for a reported $50,000 and gave the club a high-class workman at another infield position. Grimm was a fixture at first base, while various characters were appearing at second and third base. Among them was "Sparky" Adams, who had been with the club since 1922.

Adams had yet to do his best deed for the Cubs. That was to come on November 28, 1927, after the club had again finished fourth.

On the Pittsburgh Pirate roster at the time was right fielder Hazen "Kiki" Cuyler. He had helped the Pirates through the exciting world series of 1925, and it was one of his many hits which eventually gave the decision to Pittsburgh. By 1927, however, when Donie Bush had succeeded to the Pirate management, Cuyler for reasons never adequately explained was not Bush's favorite ballplayer. He appeared in but eighty-five games, and in the world series not at all. Not that it mattered much, for that was the year in which the Yankees were crashing through with one of their four-straight demonstrations in the world series, and Cuyler was probably very happy he didn't get caught in the traffic as did the playing Pirates.

McCarthy and Veeck decided to look into the Bush-Cuyler feud and paid a visit to Pittsburgh to discuss it with Barney Dreyfuss. Dreyfuss explained that Cuyler would probably be traded, since he and Bush didn't get along, but that the manager wanted infielder Hugh Critz of the Reds.

"Won't Sparky Adams do just as well?" inquired Veeck.

Dreyfuss thought he might—if outfielder Pete Scott were included. The deal was closed. It took all of five minutes but gave the Cubs an outfielder who was to become one of the delights of Wrigley Field for many years to come.

In midseason another seasoned pitcher had been obtained when Hal Carlson was secured in a trade with the Phillies. Carlson was a normal, dependable pitcher in so far as opponents and fans who watched him were concerned. He had one eccentricity, however, which trainer Andy Lotshaw discovered. Whenever it was Carl-

William Wrigley and Manager Joe McCarthy cheer Cub pennant in 1929.

son's turn to pitch, he would begin to complain of soreness in his arm. It wasn't that he was trying to avoid duty—far from it, for he was of the work-horse type. He just craved the services of the trainer and the rubbing table.

One day the Cubs were in the midst of a double-header and Carlson hadn't figured in McCarthy's original pitching plans. In between games McCarthy decided to switch to Carlson, who at once sought out trainer Lotshaw and asked for a quick rub to see if it would take out the soreness which had just developed in his arm.

Lotshaw had just started on a bottle of Coca Cola when the call came from Carlson, who had planted himself on the rubbing table, stripped to the waist. Lotshaw took a swig of the Coca Cola and approached the table carrying the bottle in his hand.

"Hal," he said, "I ain't seeming to get no place with the regular rub I been giving you. Today I got some new stuff I want to try. I hear it's mighty good."

"Try anything," said Carlson, "but hurry. I have to pitch the next game."

So, dousing the pitcher's arm and shoulder generously with the rest of the Coca Cola, Lotshaw proceeded to give Carlson a regulation rub, and sent him on his way. Carlson pitched and won his game. He was never better.

For the rest of his stay with the Cubs, until his untimely death in 1930, Carlson would have no other rub save that new stuff "Doc" Lotshaw had tried on him—but he never did find out that it was Coca Cola, that being one of the few secrets Doc Lotshaw ever kept for long.

Toward the close of the 1927 season yet another pitcher came the Cubs way. This was the left-hander, Art Nehf, who had been released unconditionally by Boston in August. Nehf had been a great pitcher for John McGraw in

New York, and his ability, his personality, and his promise even at that late stage of his career, appealed to McCarthy. The Cubs' manager guessed right on Art Nehf.

Some of McCarthy's finds were already well established with Wrigley Field patrons while the 1927 season was in progress. Hack Wilson had pounded out a .321 average to lead the club's hitters in 1926, besides getting his twenty-one home runs. Old Hoss Stephenson took charge in 1927 with a .344 average, but Hack stepped up his home-run production to thirty, and shared the league's leadership with Cy Williams of the Phillies.

Hack also led the National League that year in striking out, being fanned seventy times. If he felt too badly over this—which is unlikely—he took consolation from the fact that in the same year Babe Ruth fanned eighty-nine times against American League pitching.

The hustling, heads-up type of baseball McCarthy had them playing appealed to Chicago's fans. Attendance went to 886,925 in 1926, and in 1927 it went beyond the million mark for the first time, totaling 1,163,347.

There were other contributing factors. Wrigley and Veeck had been as active in remodeling the ball park as McCarthy was in recasting the ball club. In 1923 the lower grandstand had been subjected to reconstruction. Through 1926 and 1927 the upper deck was the object of the construction gang's efforts.

Wrigley had in mind—as has his son and successor Phillip K. Wrigley—the principle that the customer is always right. This meant that the patron who bought his way into a ball park was entitled to comfort. That comfort, believe it or not, had to include satisfaction with the caliber of baseball the Cubs were playing for him, as well as the neatness of his box, grandstand, or bleacher abiding place, or the spic and span nature of the concession stand where he might refresh himself while on the premises.

There were few complaints against the Cubs as the crowds increased to a new high through 1928. The club itself picked up momentum and took third place in the final National League standings.

At the end of the 1928 season, McCarthy, Veeck, and Wrigley, in that order, felt that one more player, preferably a strong-hitting second baseman, was needed to give the Cubs' championship stature. Such a second baseman was Rogers Hornsby, then at Boston, after a spectacular career as player and manager at St. Louis and New York.

As a member of the Cardinals, Hornsby had put together six successive National League batting championships, with averages ranging from .370 to .424. Pitchers in the league had not yet found any way to still his bat, and Hornsby himself wasn't giving any indication of being on the decline. True, he had left St. Louis after managing the Cardinals to the first world's championship of their careers. He was reported to have had trouble with the management at New York, his next abiding place. And now, all wasn't supposed to be serene at Boston, whence the Giants had sent him.

Hornsby then, was the player who might well give the Cubs that championship touch. So Veeck went forth to see what dealing could be done.

There wasn't a great deal of the "wait till I talk it over with tho boss" about Veeck or McCarthy. When the deal with Boston was proposed, Wrigley didn't expect to hear from either until it was closed. However, the deal grew in magnitude as it was discussed. Eventually Veeck felt it wise to call up Wrigley and discuss with him some of the phases of the haggling that was going on.

"You want him, don't you?" asked Wrigley.

Veeck admitted that he did.

"McCarthy wants him, doesn't he?" asked Wrigley.

Veeck said he was sure about that, too.

"Well, I certainly want him," said Wrigley. "So get him."

Never a word about probable cost. That didn't enter into Wrigley's calculations, at all.

Veeck went back and closed the deal. The record books set forth that Rogers Hornsby came to the Cubs in exchange for five players and $200,000 cash. The five players is correct. They were second baseman Freddie Maguire, catcher "Doc" Leggett, and pitchers Percy Jones, Harry Seibold, and Bruce Cunningham.

The actual cash in the transaction was $120,000 and not $200,000. However, it was a sum greater than had been paid for any other ballplayer, up to that time. The estimated value of the five players was not a great deal. They had not done much for the Cubs, and they did not combine to make the Braves any more formidable than they had been before the trade was arranged.

Thus entered into the Cub ranks one of the greatest of all National League players, in name as well as in fact.

Here was a personality the like of which the Cubs had never known before. Not all of them were to adjust themselves to Hornsby's ways at once, or ever. He was the type who said what he thought, when he thought it. As player, manager, coach, or in whatever other position he has occupied in baseball or out of it, if he liked something, he said so, and if he disliked something, he said so. But in either case what he said went. He wasn't one to retract or to apologize. In his competitive years, tact was something Hornsby hadn't learned.

The advent of Hornsby set the pennant bee buzzing in Chicago that winter and early spring. The Cubs had finished third in 1928, a bit behind the Giants, who in turn trailed the Cardinals at the finish by two games. However, the champion Cardinals had been set upon in the world series by those Yankee maulers and were slaughtered in four straight games, Babe Ruth winding up the one-sided show with three terrific homers in the fourth and final game.

It was National League history, by this time, that any one of its champions subjected to a going over in the world series by the Yankees was unlikely to recover from it in time to be much use in the following season. Pittsburgh, trounced in four straight by Ruth and Company in 1927, hadn't. So why should the Cardinals?

So the Cubs and their followers could see a pennant right ahead. No doubt Wrigley could, too, for he was with the first squad of Cubs who went to his beloved Catalina to start training that spring of 1929.

The trip across the channel was made on the *Catalina*. It was the custom of the ballplayers, or at least all of those who weren't subject to *mal de mer*, to sun themselves on the upper deck during the two hours it required to sail from the mainland to Avalon. Because of that, they were to witness an incident which had no ulterior meaning whatsoever, but which some of the veteran Cub busybodies were to remember in the days to come.

In their own way, a great many of those Cubs of the spring of 1929 had been heroes and were regarded as important as well as valuable baseball property. However, none of them had ever been invited to accompany Wrigley on the bridge of the *Catalina*. But Hornsby made it. First time out. He was up there with Wrigley and the captain of the steamer in plain sight of one and all.

Now Hornsby was the last man on that ship who would want himself to be considered the precedent-establisher.

But that's the way it was. Everybody suspected then that of all who had wanted Hornsby as a member of the champions-to-be, it was Wrigley who had wanted him most.

Though Wrigley got what he had paid for, a championship, in the very first season Hornsby was with the Cubs, the road to the pennant wasn't smooth all the way. At the very outset Gabby Hartnett, the catching mainstay, hurt his throwing arm, and he was of little use the entire season. In July the Cubs were able to make a deal with the Braves for catcher Zack Taylor, and he filled in most capably the rest of the way, when Cub power and pitching enabled the club to shake the rest of the field. The championship race ended with the Cubs ten and a half games ahead of Pittsburgh, and leading the hitters was Hornsby with .380.

Charley Root's nineteen victories and six defeats were the most productive of the league's pitching for the season, though for the Cubs' purposes Pat Malone and Guy Bush were most effective.

Hack Wilson batted in 159 runs that year. He was so eagle-eyed at the plate that he fanned but eighty-three times, as contrasted with his ninety-four of the 1928 season when he set up a mark that was going to endure until another Cub, Dolph Camilli, came along six years later to equal it.

Hack went his own way, as usual. There is no evidence that he modeled his deportment or his appetites after Hornsby, though many of the other Cubs did, especially those who were convinced that Hornsby's hitting secret was an addiction to succulent steaks.

No matter in what town Hornsby found himself, he either knew, or found out very soon where the best steak was being broiled. In Los Angeles the first spring he was with the Cubs, he discovered a lunch wagon in an otherwise vacant lot not far from the hotel at which the club stayed. He made his discovery known, and night after night the hotel's dining room was remarkably free from Cubs as they rushed to the lunch wagon to get first search on the steaks.

When you are told that in the spring-training time it is the custom for the players to sign checks, the meals being on the club when the eating is done in the hotel, you will appreciate the strain this Hornsby steak diet must have put upon them. Especially when it is known that a great many of the Cubs of that time, however great their salaries, were very cagey about parting with any money unless the emergency was grave indeed.

Whatever their dietary or monetary standards, these Cubs were a ripsnorting team which played its baseball for all it was worth. Small wonder then that Chicago went completely overboard for it, setting up a seasonal attendance record of 1,489,632.

In this highly productive season it was more of a novelty for a game to be played, weekday or Sunday, without an overflow crowd on the field than with one.

There was another new phenomenon which didn't hurt the Cubs' home attendance any: the broadcasting of the home games. Broadcasting baseball from Wrigley Field began in 1925, and was continued over the protest of some of the Cubs' rival clubs in the west, notably St. Louis.

The broadcasting of baseball out of Wrigley Field was something else again. Once started, it became a "must." At one time no less than five Chicago stations were on the air daily with the ball games. And it did help stir up trade for the Cubs, as the following figures make clear:

(1) From 1918–24 with a club that averaged fourth

place in the National League standings, the Cubs for that seven-year period drew 3,585,439 patrons.

(2) From 1925–31 with a club that averaged fourth place in the National League standings, the Cubs for that seven-year period drew 7,845,700 patrons.

That represents a gain of 119 per cent. Over the same period the other seven clubs in the league gained 27 per cent in their home attendance.

There was one other factor in the increase of interest in the Cubs and their doings at Wrigley Field: Ladies' Day. Now this gesture of setting aside an afternoon each week in which the gentler sex might watch a ball game as guests of the club had been tried by the Chicago National League club as far back as the days of Pop Anson. But until Wrigley took over the Cubs, it was more or less a gesture.

Wrigley not only invited 'em out, he practically insisted on it. Since there has never been anyone concerned with the presentation of major-league baseball wiser to the ways of promotional advertising than the Wrigleys, not even a sale of nylons in early 1946 was as productive of mass turnouts of women as were these Ladies' Days at Wrigley Field.

They were booming in 1929, but it was not until June 6, 1930, that the peak was reached. On that day there were 51,556 persons in Wrigley Field, whose normal capacity wasn't quite 40,000. Of that 51,556 persons, 30,476 were ladies, guests of the management.

It was in this 1929 setting, and with that 1929 ball club that Wrigley gained his first objective, a National League championship. That was only half the battle. What Wrigley wanted most was a world's championship. And that, the Cubs set out to try to get for him on October 8, the series opening in Chicago.[1]

Fred Lieb describes the Series between the Cubs and A's:

Connie Mack dazed the sports world, also his own players, by pitching long, angular Howard Ehmke, now a Philadelphia manufacturer of tarpaulin infield covers, in the first game of the series in Chicago, October 8, 1929. Ehmke, formerly a great pitcher, then was thirty-five and near the end of his career. During the 1929 season he had appeared in only 11 games, pitched a total of 55 innings, equivalent to 6 nine-inning games, had a record of 7 games won and 2 lost, but worked only 2 complete games.

Only in recent years has Mack told the real story of how he came to pitch Ehmke in the first game, and that for over two weeks before the series it was a secret between Ehmke and himself that the tall right-hander would draw the opening assignment in Chicago.

Shortly before the Athletics left on their last Western trip, Mack called Ehmke to his little office in Shibe Park. "Howard, there comes a time in everyone's life when there has to be a change, and I think we've reached the point where we soon must part company."

"All right, Mr. Mack. If that is the way it is, it has to be," said the pitcher. "I haven't helped you much this year, and it's lucky you didn't need me. But I've always wanted to pitch in a World's Series, and I'd like to work in the series, if only for a few innings."

Then Ehmke flexed his arm like a prize fighter and remarked: "I think I've got one more good game left in there."

"So do I," agreed Connie. "Now, you needn't make our last western trip, but stay in the East and catch the Cubs in Philadelphia and New York. See what they like to hit, make notes on them; for I am going to pitch you in the first game."

The night before the first game, it was whispered in the Chicago press room that Mack would pitch Ehmke, the 55-inning pitcher, against Charley Root, McCarthy's top man. The sports writers grinned—it was just Connie trying to confuse Marse Joe. Both of Mack's aces, Grove and Earnshaw, expected to get the call and were surprised that Connie hadn't spoken to either of them.

As the players reached Wrigley Field, and Ehmke left the bench, he must have had doubts that Mack would carry out his September plan. "Is it still me?" he asked.

"Yes, Howard, it still is you."

When it came nearly time for the pitchers to warm up, Earnshaw, of his own accord, started to toss a few pitches to Cy Perkins. Then Ehmke took off his windbreaker to warm up, and there was a little grumbling on the Athletic bench.

"Are you going to let that guy pitch?" Simmons asked Mack, half belligerently.

"Yes, I am, Al," Connie replied quietly.

The great outfielder started to say something, but quickly thought better of it. "Well, if he's your selection, it's all right with me," he said.

Ehmke, warming up for the Athletics, threw the stands, especially the press box, into utter confusion; and Connie—with that twinkle in his eye—thoroughly enjoyed it. "Why, they tell me that Bob Quinn, who then was president of the Red Sox, almost fainted in his box," Mack laughed, relating the incident. In the press stand they were asking: "Has the old man gone screwy, soft in the head or something?"

Probably even Mack could not have suspected the game Ehmke still had tucked away in his arm, for How-

ard pitched one of the World's Series classics. Before
that autumn afternoon was over, Ehmke had established
a new World's Series strike-out record of 13. It was an
unusually warm day for Chicago in October, and the
fans in the center field bleachers were in their shirt
sleeves. Pitching side arm from his right hip, Howard
kept the ball concealed from the Chicago batsmen and
then let the Cubs lose it in that bleacher background.
The Cubs got 8 hits to 6 for the A's, but Chicago didn't
score until the ninth, when they were helped by Dykes's
two-base wild throw.

For six innings Charley Root fought off Ehmke on
even terms, but in the seventh inning that broth of a boy
from the Eastern Shore, Jimmy Foxx, brought joy to Connie and grief to the Chicago stands by driving a homer
into the center-field bleachers. Root retired in the second half, so pinch-hitter Gabby Hartnett might strike
out for him, and the A's closed with two runs on Guy
Bush in the ninth. A pair of errors by Woodie English,
McCarthy's shortstop, set the stage for the Philadelphia
tallies and brought a successful outcome to Mack's great
pitching gamble.

"I've thought since what people might have said if I
had lost that game—with Earnshaw, Grove, and Walberg
sitting on my bench," said Connie.

"It's your turn tomorrow, George," Connie said smil-
ingly to Earnshaw, after Ehmke had completed his brilliant first-game victory.

The second game, also played in Chicago, was another
"lovely day" for Mr. McGillicuddy, even though he had
to remove Earnshaw during a Cub rally in the fifth inning. However, between the "Big Moose" and Grove, his
successor, the famous pair matched Ehmke's 13 strike-
outs of the first game. The A's hit Pat Malone and a com-

pany of relief men, Sheriff Blake, Hal Carlson and Art Nehf, with everything—including the kitchen stove. Foxx and Simmons, both of whom hit homers, were especially devastating, driving in seven runs between them. Jimmy started the Athletic scoring parade in the third, when his second round-tripper in two days followed a single by Cochrane and a walk to Simmons.

The final score was Athletics, 9; Cubs, 3. Mack was letting his mind revert back to the series with Chance's Cubs nineteen years before. The two series were running a strange parallel. The score of the first 1929 victory was almost the same as Bender's opening victory of 1910, which was 4 to 1. The second games of both series produced the same score—9 to 3. It boded well for a new Athletic World's Championship.

The Cubs finally bagged a game, winning the third contest by a score of 3 to 1. Earnshaw again was good, struck out ten men, and gave up only six hits against nine off Guy Bush, his opponent. But the Cubs ganged up on Connie's Moose in the sixth, scoring their three runs on singles by Hornsby and Cuyler, a walk for Bush and a fumble by Dykes.

If Connie can chuckle over winning the first game with his mystery pitcher, Ehmke, his face expands into a broad grin when he recalls his Columbus Day victory in the fourth encounter. "Yes, we surely put over a beautiful rally that afternoon," he admits, "and if we hadn't scored those ten runs in the seventh inning, I was prepared to put in the biggest bunch of rookies anyone ever saw at a World's Series game. I had planned to put every substitute on my bench in the game the last two innings."

With the possible exception of the last game of the 1906 World Series, which Frank Chance's club lost to the Hitless Wonder White Sox, 8 to 3, the loss of that Columbus Day game—after piling up an 8 to 0 lead for Charley Root, McCarthy's ace—was the most painful defeat in the sixty-eight-year history of the Chicago National League club.

Mack opened the game with old Jack Quinn, the veteran spitballer, who held off Root for three innings. The Cubs reached old Jack for two runs in the fourth, and then shelled him out in the sixth, rolling over five runs as Connie rushed in Walberg and then Rommel. Eddie gave up Chicago's eighth run in the first half of the seventh, and the Philadelphia fans yawned. It looked like the worst Athletic World's Series defeat since Matty beat Andy Coakley, 9 to 0, in 1905.

The Athletics had made only three hits off Root, and there was only a ripple of enthusiasm in the Philadelphia dugout when Simmons opened the A's half of the seventh with a lusty home-run clout to the roof of the left-field stand. "Well, we won't be shut out, anyway," Jimmy Dykes said to Connie, hoping to contribute a little optimism to the general gloom.

However, the homer seemingly touched off a rally, as Foxx, Bing Miller, and Dykes each paddled out singles, bringing in a second run. As Boley started for the plate, Connie began to take a real interest in the rally. "I think that fellow has lost his stuff," he said. "Swing at the first good one you see, Joe, and hit it."

Boley followed instructions to the letter, and his single fetched in Miller. There was a lull in the rally as George Burns, batting for Rommel, popped to Shortstop English; but, when little Bishop also cracked out a single, scoring Dykes, the entire Athletic bench jumped into action. The Elephants had cut the Chicago lead in half, and still had two runners on base.

McCarthy didn't like the way things were going; he dismissed Root and called in Art Nehf, the former Giant left-hander, to pitch to Mule Haas, a left-handed batter. Mule hit a screeching line drive to center, but a ball which was playable. But Hack Wilson, the Cub center fielder, misjudged it badly. He first started to come in for the ball, then apparently was blinded by the sun and lost the sphere completely. It cleared his head and rolled out to deep center field, as Stephenson ran over from left to retrieve it.

Boley and Bishop scored, and then "the Donk," too, was waved in from third by Coach Eddie Collins. "He's goin' to make it! He's goin' to make it!" yelled the excited Dykes. Then, giving the next player to him on the bench a resounding slap on the back, Jimmy cried: "We're back in the game, gang!"

However, Jimmy didn't smack a fellow player, but the tall lean tactician himself. In the excitement Connie had gotten up and sat next to Dykes. He was leaning forward, watching Mule's slide, and Jimmy's vigorous thump knocked him off the bench and out among the bats. Again it was 1910 all over again.

"I'm sorry, terribly sorry," said Jimmy, reaching out to give his boss a hand.

"It's all right, Jimmy. Everything's all right," said Connie. "In fact, anything you do is all right. And isn't this a wonderful rally?"

Haas's three-run gift homer reduced the Cub lead to 8 to 7. McCarthy didn't blame Nehf and let him stay in long enough to walk Cochrane. Joe then switched to Sheriff Blake, a right-hander, but in a jiffy Simmons and Foxx—up for the second time—both bumped out singles, and the score was tied at 8 to 8. McCarthy was getting desperate and now called in Pat Malone, who promptly plunked Bing Miller in the ribs, filling the bases.

Here was another laugh! Runs had scored so fast that Jimmy Dykes had lost track of them; he thought the A's still were a run behind and went up to swing from his hip, hoping to bring in what he thought to be the tying run from third with a long fly. He hit a fast ball and pulled it to left. But it went beyond Jim's expectations. Stephenson jumped for the ball, got his fingertips on it, but couldn't hold it; it went for a double, as the joyful Simmons and Foxx streamed over the plate. Malone then struck out Boley and Burns, the pinch-hitter providing two of the putouts of the inning; but the A's now were ahead, 10 to 8.

During the big rally, Connie had called to Grove, "Get yourself ready, Bob." Mose tried to watch the game from the bull pen and warm up at the same time. But when he came in he surely was ready. In the eighth and ninth innings he retired the six Cubs who faced him as fast as they came up, striking out four of them.

In his fifth game Mack again started Ehmke, but without the element of surprise and the help of that Chicago bleacher Howard wasn't the pitcher he had been in the opener at Wrigley Field. Connie took him out during a Cub rally which netted McCarthy two runs in the fourth. From there on, big Rube Walberg pitched shutout ball; but, as the Athletics had been helpless before Pat Malone for eight innings, it again looked like a Cub victory and a trip back to Chicago for a sixth, and possible seventh, game. Up to the ninth, big Pat had a two-hit shutout in his grasp.

But Connie's 1929 boys just didn't know how to lose. The inning started inauspiciously enough when Walter

French, the West Pointer, struck out for Walberg. But Bishop set a new rally into motion with a single to left; and Mule Haas, one of the heroes of the previous game's explosion, set off a new bomb under McCarthy's bench. He sent a beautiful line-drive home run sailing over the right-field wall for a clout which tied the score.

When the cheering on the Athletic bench abated, Connie grinned and remarked to the Donk: "Well, George, they can't say Wilson misjudged that one."

More fireworks were to come for Connie and his fans. Hornsby threw out Cochrane for the second out, but Simmons hit the top of the right-field scoreboard with a dynamic double, the ball bouncing back into the playing field. Had the ball gone to the right or left of the scoreboard, which extended beyond the fence, it would have ended the game then and there. The honor of driving in the winning run was left to Bing Miller. With the count two balls and two strikes, he, too, rifled the ball against the scoreboard, as Simmons, with big loping steps, tore in with the run which made Mack the World's Champion manager again after a period of sixteen years. He also became the first to win four blue ribbons; previously he had been tied with McGraw and Huggins with three.

After the game, Joe McCarthy, the Philadelphia boy, came into the Athletic clubhouse and offered his congratulations.

"You've a great fighting team, Connie," said Joe.

"And I'm glad I don't have to play against your right-handed hitters all season," said Mack.

Despite Connie's dislike for vulgarity and rough stuff in baseball "riding," the two clubs had been pretty crude in their conversation in the early games of the series. The Cubs had some pretty good jockeys in Pat Malone,

Guy Bush, Charley Root, Wilson, Hartnett, and Grimm; and the A's—with their Cochrane, Haas, Dykes, and Rommel—weren't exactly baseball sissies. They gave back what they received and tried to add a little interest.

It reached such a point that Judge Landis called the two managers, Mack and McCarthy, to his quarters and said: "If this indecent language doesn't stop, I will fine the players guilty of it a full share. Often it is difficult to tell who is yelling. In that case, I will fine the manager."

Mack called a meeting in his clubhouse and brusquely announced: "From now on, all jockeying is off. I'll not hear another word of it."

Prior to the last game, Cochrane yelled at the silenced Cubs:

"After this game, we'll serve tea in the clubhouse."

Mack was afraid this had reached the Commissioner's ears. "Do you want it to cost you money, Mickey?" he asked.

However, when Landis came into the Athletic clubhouse to congratulate the victors, he threw his arms around the happy Cochrane and said: "Now let's have that tea."

Connie escaped from the clubhouse as soon as he could. Rud Rennie, the observing *New York Herald Tribune* baseball writer, followed the grand old leader. Office girls kissed and hugged him as he made his way to his own private office in the tower. He stood for a few minutes like a man in a daze, his fingertips shaking against his hips.

"You must excuse me a minute," he said. "I am afraid I overdid it a bit."

Then he lay down on a low leather couch and pressed his hands against his throbbing temples. Nearing sixty-seven, the excitement of those last two games was beyond anything he had experienced.[2]

As for the Cubs, 1929 turned out to be a depression in more ways than one.

—4—

WITH PENNANTS FLYING

No one is better qualified to tell the story of the Cubs in the 1930s and '40s than Charlie Grimm. Those were happy times for the Cubs thanks in no small measure to Jolly Cholly. **The following edited selections are from his book,** ***Grimm's Baseball Tales:***

We made no major changes for 1930, but the best way to describe the mood of the fans and the executives, from William Wrigley on down, was that we were all suffering from a hangover from the World Series. Instead of being heroes, we were now vulnerable to our followers when things went wrong. But it was a good season, and the only reason we didn't repeat as champions, I'm sure, was because Hornsby suffered an ankle fracture late in May. He played in only forty-two games that season and batted .308. This was the beginning of the end for him as a player. He played one hundred games in 1931, but that was the last of Rog as an effective ball player.

Wilson, far from losing his cool after those baffling seconds under Philadelphia's blazing sun, came back in 1930 for his most terrific season. He hit fifty-six homers, still high in the National League. He boosted across 190 runs, a Major League mark I'll gamble will never be topped. And, down there in the fine print, you'll note that he walked 105 times. He made 198 hits, and exclusive of reaching base by being hit or through an error, Hack was a base runner 303 times! Candor forces me to add that the little round man was charged with nineteen errors, which isn't good for an outfielder.

Despite the injury to Hornsby and the loss of his big bat, we finished second, losing out only because Gabby Street's Cardinals made a whirlwind finish to beat us by two games.

But, before the championship was decided, McCarthy was out of the picture. On September 23 Hornsby was elevated to the big job. I never knew the full story, but it probably started developing after that ten-run Philadelphia inning. Wrigley was a proud man, and a World Series championship was his goal. Marse Joe completed the season after Wrigley announced that Hornsby would be the leader in 1931.

A reporter asked Wrigley to explain the move.

"Since the day I entered baseball as an owner I have had my heart set on winning a World Series," W.W. said. "It may be that we will be worse off if the change is made and the move may not be popular with the fans. McCarthy was given free rein in the buying of players and I believe we have a great team. McCarthy has had five years to prove this, so I don't think there's anything unusual about not engaging him after a stretch such as that."

Reporters looked deeper into it. "McCarthy had delegated Joe Tinker [the old-time Cub star shortstop] to scout the Athletics in the World Series," one wrote. "Tinker advised inside pitches to Al Simmons and Mickey Cochrane. Hornsby insisted they should be pitched on the outside. And later in the series the pitchers followed Hornsby's line."

There also was the usual charge, and it has never died down, that the Cubs in 1930 were victims of over-adulation after their 1929 pennant—too many social engagements to the detriment of performance on the field.

Before the Wrigley announcement there had been reports that McCarthy and Hornsby were feuding because the Rajah had not been playing regularly.

"When the Cubs were at home on Sunday, September 7, Hornsby was out of the lineup," wrote Irving Vaughan in the *Chicago Tribune*. "On this day his legs were in such condition that he could move only with difficulty. He told McCarthy he was hurting and suggested he had better rest, but would play if Joe wanted it that way."

After Hornsby walked away, McCarthy turned to Vaughan and said: "I'm glad you were here to hear this because, in a couple of days, you'll be reading that I kept him on the bench to embarrass him."

Sure enough, the stories appeared as Joe had predicted.

Anyway, now W.W. had Hornsby up there at the head of his baseball empire. This was the man he had ordered be obtained at any cost. When Rog took command of the Cubs on Catalina Island in 1931 he was thirty-five years old. He was still imperious, icy, and imperturbable, and he never changed, in victory or defeat.

McCarthy, I've always thought, realized his number was up after we blew that 1929 series. My old friend Warren Brown, who still is banging the typewriter keys, had a wide acquaintanceship in sports, and his judgment was highly respected. And Warren, between writing columns for the old *Chicago Herald-Examiner*, paved the way, as a contact man with owner Jake Ruppert, for McCarthy to become manager of the Yankees in 1931. Marse Joe was to come back to Wrigley Field the next year, very definitely in the visitors' dugout.

There were no dramatic personnel changes for Rog's 1931 season. The biggest deal, as I remember it, was a $50,000 check to owner Emil Fuchs of the Braves for Bob Smith, a pretty good pitcher who originally had been an infielder. He was 15–12 for us, but was far from the answer for a pennant. We also bought Jakie May, a lefty, from the Reds, and Les (Sugar) Sweetland from the Phils. This wasn't enough, either. We had high hopes that Ed Baecht, up from our Los Angeles club, would lead us on high, but he was a bust. We finished third, 15½ games behind the Cardinals.

Wilson, who had worn out pitchers in the two previous seasons, went into a shocking decline. I think he missed the soothing influence of McCarthy. This is not to downgrade Hornsby. Managers are of different types. Marse Joe could get maximum performance out of Hack. Perhaps Hornsby's tactics with other players would pay off better against McCarthy's style.

At any rate, Hack tapered off to .261 in 112 games, missing more than forty. He hit only thirteen homers and batted in sixty-one runs, in stark contrast to his sensational 1930.

Hornsby, doubling as a player, had his final big season, hitting .331 in one hundred games and knocking sixteen homers. He was bothered by a spur on his heel. Often he played in pain. Those days when he didn't start, he'd go up as a pinch batter, usually taunted by the fans, who, with great hindsight, wished that McCarthy was still calling the shots.

The biggest news of 1931 came when Wilson, one of Wrigley's Field's all-time favorites, was traded to the Cardinals at season's end. This wasn't a new story. It had happened many times before to great players. Few start and finish with the same ball club. Now the Cubs were trading their all-time greatest slugger to the Cardinals for Burleigh Grimes, a veteran right-hander and one of the last of the spitballers. In 1931, Grimes, thirty-eight years old, had won 5 out of 5 from the Cubs while progressing toward a 17–9 record. He had won the third game of the World Series against the Athletics and had taken the seventh and final game, with help from Wild Bill Hallahan.

In that season, Grimes was drawing $18,000, the highest figure on the Cards' payroll. Wilson was in the $35,000 bracket, but in those days the club owners were not restrained from slashing a player's salary from year to year; today's maximum cut is 25 per cent. It was agreed by all that Hack's pay would be brutally carved.

Hack was bitter, charging that Hornsby would not let him hit on the 3 and 0 or the 3 and 1 counts. "I had to take a lot of sweet strikes I might have hammered out of the lot," he complained. Before the season started, the Cardinals traded Hack to the Dodgers for $40,000 and a rookie outfielder named Bob Parham.

At Hornsby's insistence, the Cubs bought Lance Richbourg, an outfielder, from the Braves, but he wasn't to do much in 1932. And neither was Rog, who played in only nineteen games, including some service in the outfield, but mostly as a pinch batter—when he had the supreme confidence he still could hit the ball if it meant something. Sometimes he did.

Without a doubt, 1932 was the newsiest of all my Cub years. Long before the championship was decided and we went into the World Series against Babe Ruth and his Yankee pals, the public pulse had been tapped to a pulp. And not everything happened on the field.

There was a stately old hotel within walking distance

of Wrigley Field, called the Carols. In the thirties it was
the summer home of many of our players. In 1932, twenty-
four-year-old Bill Jurges had become our regular shortstop. He really could play the position and he had a rifle
arm. He was going strong in mid-season, a new personality on the club.

Athletes, especially the non-attached ones, always have
been, and will continue to be, targets of young romantic
ladies. Bill, a handsome fellow, had caught the attention
of a show girl carrying the extensive name of Violet Pop-
ovitch Heindel-Valli. Without regard to our next game,
she invaded the hotel, plunked Bill in the ribs and left
hand, then added a superficial bullet wound for herself.
Bill recovered to become one of baseball's greatest short-
stops. He declined to sign a complaint. And Violet went
on dancing, without her gun.

As the 1932 season progressed, I had a feeling that
Veeck and Hornsby didn't hit it off. There was no shouting, but just an undercurrent we all felt. Veeck had waved
the pennant flag before the season started. The hard-
bitten Hornsby, knowing all the pitfalls ahead for even
the greatest of teams in the long season, was less opti-
mistic. It probably didn't help Rog's ego that Richbourg
had failed to be a big gun. Hornsby had been encour-
aged with the development of Jurges and Billy Herman,
which gave us a terrific middle of the infield combination. Rog also had been pleasantly surprised by the hitting of Riggs Stephenson. But, still, he didn't make any
rosy predictions.

I think it got down to Hornsby becoming bored with
Veeck's championship claims and with Veeck finally getting tired of Hornsby emphasizing our shortcomings. I'll
always believe this was the main problem and that the
horse-betting charges that followed had little or nothing

to do with the decision that Rog had to go and that I would become the manager.

This was like the irrestible force colliding with an immovable object. William Wrigley had called Veeck the best of the baseball executives. He also had said that Hornsby was the "smartest baseball manager and player that ever lived."

Now the time had come to separate the two. The break came after we lost to the Dodgers in Ebbets Field 4 to 3, when Johnny Fredericks beat us with a home run on August 2. It put us five games behind the Pirates. We left New York early that evening for Philadelphia, and Rog was not on the train. We checked into the Benjamin Franklin Hotel and Bob Lewis knocked at my door and said Veeck wanted to see me right away.

"What did I do now?" I asked Bob.

I went up to Veeck's suite and, before he had a chance to say anything, I asked: "What's up?"

He didn't mince words. He said he wanted me to manage the Cubs. "But you have a manager," I said.

"Hornsby doesn't live here anymore," said my host. Only then did it dawn on me that Hornsby was out.

So I accepted.

Later, I called the players to my room. Rollie Hemsley, one of the catchers, made a flowery speech. I knew why he was so sweet. He and Hornsby never did get along. Well, the boys finally went their way. Rollie was the first to break the midnight curfew rule, but he salvaged his career in later years by staying away from the speakeasies and taverns. Stan Hack was the No. 2 offender in my new regime, but he'd come up the next day and confess.

The next morning I saw Hornsby in the hotel lobby and told him I had accepted only after I'd been assured that he was out. The Rajah seemed gracious, but this wasn't the last I was to hear from him about the switch. Rog signed on with his old club, the Cardinals, and when we came into St. Louis early in the 1933 season I was boiling after hearing that he had accused me of undermining him with the Cubs.

I was in a mood to go into the Cardinals' dressing room and have it out with him. Fortunately for all concerned, Veeck was with us on the trip, and he calmed me down. Hornsby had felt bad when the Cubs failed to vote him a full share of the 1932 World Series money. I had nothing to do with it, because managers were excluded when the pie was cut.

Much later, there were no hard feelings when we were elderly coaches for the Cubs in Arizona. Rog and I would walk from the hotel to Rendezvous Park in Mesa. He was a lonely man, but I always thought he enjoyed being alone with his thoughts, whether helping out on the field or decorating the lobby in an easy chair. I have nothing but kind feelings for him. In 1915, when I was selling popcorn in old Robinson Field in St. Louis, I saw him when he came up to the Cardinals. I remember that the scout who signed him, Bob Connery, said that Rog was going to be a great one. Little did I know then that one day we'd be controversial figures 'way up there in the big time.

Billy Herman took over Hornsby's vacated spot at second base. Except for this move, there were no lineup changes. We started winning and the Pirates cooled off. On August 11 we went to Pittsburgh for a single game, winning it to take a half-game lead. We stayed in front the rest of the way, clinching the flag in Wrigley Field on September 20. Cuyler's triple with the bases loaded broke a tie with the Pirates in the seventh and helped Bush win his nineteenth game. After the final out, Guy

ran over to me to get the ball for his souvenir cabinet.
That day, I remember, the Cubs' stock jumped 85 points
to 350, but there were no shares available. A month before, it was quoted at around 200 and early in the season
was only 125. In 1929 Cub stock soared to 550. Only
about 10 per cent of the stock was on the market.

One of our surprise helpers to the championship was
Mark Koenig, earlier a star shortstop with the Yankees.
He was playing in the Pacific Coast League when we
bought him after the shooting of Jurges. A great home
stand in August, when we won eighteen out of twenty,
many of them late-inning sizzlers, brought us the top
spot by four games. Right up there helping us win was
Koenig, who was twenty-eight at the time. He batted
.353 for us in thirty-three games and drove across seventeen runs, many of them for the winning margin.

I was disappointed when I learned Koenig had been
voted only half a share of the World Series money to
come against Joe McCarthy's Yankees. Commissioner
Landis was downright indignant and he summoned me
to his office.

"You can tell your boys that everybody feels bad about
them voting Koenig only a one-half share and that they
won't get their World Series checks until next January,"
he snapped.

This was his way of punishing the players, whom the
Yankees were to label "cheapskates" in the forthcoming
series.

The ball started bouncing for us the first day Mark
put on a Cub uniform. He did everything right and turned
out to be a leader in the field. The Yankees turned Koenig
into a psychological weapon against us in the series with
their taunts at this tight-fisted injustice to their old pal.

Our big new pitching star of 1932 was Lon (Dick)

Warneke, a gangling twenty-three-year-old right-hander from the Ozarks. He had come full flower in this season, winning 22 and losing only 6. He went all the way twenty-six times in thirty-five starts and had a 2.37 earned run average in 277 innings. Bush won 19 out of 30, Root was 15–10, but Malone dropped off to 15–17. Grimes, now thirty-eight, lost 11 out of 16. Bud Tinning, Bob Smith, and Jakie May helped.

I had played in 149 games, batting .307 and driving in eighty runs. We had started the season with Stan Hack, a rookie and ex-Sacramento bank clerk, at third base. Then there was a shift, with English taking over at third, mainly because Jurges had better range than Woody. Stephenson still was in left, Cuyler in right. Johnny Moore and Frank Demaree were platooned in center. Stevie led us with .324, but this was far from being the explosive team of 1929. Lefty O'Doul, the man the Cubs couldn't see in 1926, hit .368 for the Dodgers to win the batting crown.

The series opened in Yankee Stadium. It was Bush against Charley Ruffing, who had been 18–7 for the Yankees. Guy was perfect the first three innings, and we jumped off with a two-run lead. Herman and English singled and when Ruth bobbled the ball, Billy scored. Stephenson singled to bring in English.

Lou Gehrig, Ruth's junior partner, who was to be the hitting standout of the series, hit a three-run homer in the fourth after a pass to Earle Combs and Ruth's single. The Yankees knocked out Bush in a five-run sixth. Guy walked the first three, and Bill Dickey singled for two runs. After giving up a fourth walk, Bush yielded to Grimes and Combs singled for the final two runs of the inning. The final score was 12 to 6.

The second game matched Warneke against Vernon

(Lefty) Gomez, the great young southpaw who had won twenty-four and lost only seven during the season. Again we rushed into a lead when Herman led with a first-inning double and scored on Stephenson's fly.

Now Warneke made his World Series debut. When he walked Combs and little Joey Sewell, the infielders, including myself, went over to calm him down. Lon fanned Ruth, but Gehrig singled to tie the score. The Yankees went ahead to stay when Dickey singled. In the third, Stephenson doubled and Demaree singled for our last run. But the Yanks came back in their half when Ben Chapman drove in two runs with a single. In the fifth, Gehrig knocked his third hit and scored the game's final run on Dickey's single. That made it 5 to 2, and it was back to Chicago for the conclusion of the sad story.

We started Root against George Pipgras, a right-hander who had a 16–9 record. Ruth and Gehrig started putting on a home run show in the first inning. Combs was safe on a high throw by Jurges, Sewell walked, and the Babe hit one into the right-field seats with nobody out. We got one back in our portion, small solace to the overflow crowd of 49,986, when Herman walked and Cuyler doubled against the screen in right.

Gehrig led in the third with a homer into the right-field seats, but we came back with two right away on a homer by Cuyler, a single by Stephenson, and my double, which scored Moore, who had forced the Old Hoss. We tied it in the fourth when Jurges doubled, advanced on Root's infield out, and scored after Frank Crosetti booted English's grounder.

All this time a noisy battle of words was mounting from the rival dugouts. This brings us up to Ruth's famous visit to the plate with one out in the fifth inning. Bush, leading the tirade from our bench, turned a blast

on the Babe. One of the nicknames he didn't like was
"Big Monkey," and I'm sure Guy included it. Even before
Root got over his first of two pitches for strikes, Babe
pointed straight away and turned toward our dugout—
no doubt for Bush's benefit. Those who saw Ruth's pointing finger chose to believe, when he drove the ball over
the center-field bleachers, that he was calling his shot.

I hesitate to spoil a good story, one that has been built
up to such proportions down the years that millions of
people have insisted they saw the gesture, but the Babe
actually was pointing to the mound. As he pointed, I
heard Ruth growl: "You'll be out there tomorrow—so we'll
see what you can do with me, you so-and-so tightwad!"

Well, the next day, Ruth didn't hit any homers off Bush.
He was plunked by a pitched ball the only time he faced
the Mississippi Mudcat, who didn't have the stuff that
day, lasting only a third of an inning.

Root never squawked as the legend grew that Ruth
had called his shot for baseball's most celebrated home
run. But he did balk when he was offered a chunk of
money to recreate the scene in the Babe Ruth movie
made later in Hollywood. If old Chinski could have called
back any one of the thousands of pitches he made for the
Cubs, the one Ruth picked on would have been his choice.
Let's face it, though, a great guy hit that homer, the greatest slugger of all time. And if you want to believe he
really planned it that way, you just go right ahead!

After Ruth's bomb, Gehrig followed with a homer to
right and I turned the pitching over to Malone. The
game settled down after that, ending in a 7 to 5 Yankee
triumph.

The Yankees came back the next afternoon to complete their four-game sweep. Poor Guy never could get
untracked. After Combs and Sewell singled, Ruth was

hit on the arm. Combs scored on Gehrig's fly and when Tony Lazzeri walked, Warneke took over.

Johnny Allen, the Yankees' hard-throwing right-hander, couldn't last out the first inning, either, when we scored four runs, three on Demaree's homer. We batted around, old Wilcey Moore getting Warneke for the third out.

In the third, Gehrig doubled and Lazzeri hit a homer. The ball landed on top of the wire fence in right field and bounced into the stands. In the sixth, Gehrig hit a two-run single, but we tied it in our half. I was safe when Moore dropped the ball on my bouncer to Gehrig and later scored when Crosetti threw the ball into the Yankee dugout on Hartnett's grounder.

But the Yankees knocked out Jakie May in the seventh, scoring four times. They repeated in the ninth and made it 13 to 6.

Gehrig had hit .529, hitting three homers, scoring nine runs, and driving in eight. It was Ruth's final World Series. Our only consistent hitter was Stephenson, who plugged Yankee pitching for .444. William Wrigley didn't live to suffer through those four rough afternoons. He had passed away earlier in the year, on January 26.

After winning the National League title in 1932, we were on the three-year pennant plan, but we didn't know it. The pattern had started in 1929. It continued when we made it to the top in 1935 and 1938, the year I stepped aside for Gabby Hartnett.

We had won in 1929 after bringing in Hornsby. Despite our championship in 1932, we weren't satisfied with our attack. We had no phenoms coming up from the Minors, but there still was a lively market with rival clubs who were dazzled by cash offers, especially in those depression years. So we started shopping for another slugger, though we knew there were no Hornsbys around. A

$75,000 poultice, plus four players, was gratefully accepted by the Cincinnati Reds in exchange for the so-called Daffy Dodger, Floyd (Babe) Herman. We made this deal for the 1933 season, garnishing the cash with Bob Smith, Rollie Hemsley, Johnny Moore, and Lance Richbourg.

Babe, an angular Californian who batted left, had hit .381 for the Dodgers in 1929, but O'Doul clubbed .398. The next year Herman batted .390, but he again was an also-ran for the title when Bill Terry of the Giants hit .401.

Herman was "crazy like a fox." He was a big, good-natured fellow who might have become "teched in the head" by association with the other Dodgers, including Uncle Wilbert Robinson, the manager. Despite his flair for sometimes gumming up a ball game and playing the great Dumbo part, Babe was (and still is) a shrewd man.

Babe's daffiness tag came through no fault of his own. The bases were filled when he came to bat in a game in Brooklyn's Ebbets Field in 1926. Hank DeBerry was on third, Dazzy Vance on second, and Chick Fewster on first. Babe singled to right, scoring DeBerry, but Vance, fearing the ball would be caught, held up at third. Fewster fled around second and headed for third. Herman, figuring he had knocked an extra baser for sure, raced past mid-diamond. All three wound up on third base. Babe retreated toward second base. Fewster, thinking he was automatically out, stepped off third and was tagged. The ball was thrown to second base in time to double Herman.

During one game when Herman was out with an injury, a Pirate drove the ball into the left-field corner, out of Manager Robinson's view. He asked Babe what had happened.

"I don't know, Robbie," he answered. "I was reading

the paper." It was on his lap, opened to the sports section. Babe was making headway convincing the chroniclers he had been pegged wrong as an eccentric until the time he plucked a cigar butt out of his coat pocket. He put it to his mouth and started fumbling for a match.

"Light?" asked a reporter.

Babe drew in his breath a few times and said: "Never mind, it's lit."

We just didn't have it in 1933, but it wasn't Herman's fault. He batted .289 and knocked in 93 runs. It was with the Cubs that he had his biggest thrill when he blasted three homers in St. Louis in one day off the Dean brothers, Dizzy and Paul. We finished third, five games behind the Giants and only one back of the Pirates. Hard times really were upon us. We played to only 595,000 spectators, a drop of almost 400,000 from the previous season. And, as the 1933 season drew to a close, William Veeck passed away. Baseball had lost two great men in two years.

We made another effort to buy a pennant, looking toward 1934. Chuck Klein of the Phillies, a southpaw slugger, had won the National League title with a .368 average in 1933, hitting twenty-eight homers and driving in 120 runs.

Klein had been a terror for the Phillies, but he had two big things going for him. He was playing for a lowly club and he had a short right-field target in Baker Bowl. Now he was coming to a contender and would face superior pitching. And the fences would be more difficult to reach in Chicago.

Klein was ours for $65,000 plus Mark Koenig, pitcher Ted Kleinhans, and Harvey Hendrick. The deal was made late in November of 1933, and Chuck, who lived in Indiana, was brought to Chicago for a press conference.

William H. (Bill) Walker had taken over as president of the Cubs. He was a large florid man and more a baseball enthusiast than an executive.

When the stage was set for Klein's grand entrance, a young man entered the room. Walker stepped toward the visitor enthusiastically, calling out "Chuck!" But it wasn't Chuck at all. He got there later.

I lost count of how many times Bill Walker fired me in the 1934 season, but I guess all I'd have to do to find out is to look up how many games we lost. He balanced it, I guess, by inviting me out to dinner after each victory. Walker was the butt of some of the newspapermen, notably the sometimes fiendish Warren Brown of the *Herald-Examiner*. Once, when the Cardinals were in Wrigley Field for a series, Warren wrote this little paragraph:

"Bill Walker will start on the mound today for the Cardinals. This Bill Walker isn't to be confused with the Cubs' Bill Walker, who is confused enough as it is."

Now, 1934 was quite a year, even though we were outdistanced. The Cubs again were third, trailing Frank Frisch's Cardinals by eight games, the Giants by six.

It was the year of the Cub first basemen, you might say. I had been bothered by back trouble for years and knew that I couldn't go on forever, so we were looking for help in this position. It just so happened that in June of 1934 we had two youngsters who were to become among the game's greatest at the position. One of them, Dolph Camilli, got away. The other one, Phil Cavarretta, stayed to become not only a star but a Cub manager.

We brought Camilli up from Sacramento that spring. And just as soon as Cavarretta accepted his diploma at Chicago's Lane Tech High School, he reported to us in Wrigley Field. He had hit a ball out of the park on his first swing in a tryout. Phil had also pitched in high

Jolly Cholly Grimm who helped the Cubs to five pennants as a
player and manager.

school. When I first saw him I was impressed with the vitality of the slim, grim-faced eighteen-year-old. He had such all-around ability, plus his great desire, that I decided right away he should forget pitching and become an everyday performer. He was to knock me off first base and play 146 games, batting .276, when we won the title in 1935. And he also was quite an outfielder.

Dolph Camilli was our regular first baseman when the season started and was doing fairly well about the time that Cavarretta joined us. One mid-June afternoon when we were idle, I took my family to the Century of Progress on the lakefront. We had just returned to my apartment when the phone rang. The reporter wanted to know if it was true we had swapped Camilli to the Phillies for Don Hurst, also a first baseman.

This was one of life's embarrassing moments. I didn't know if it had happened. Had I said it was news to me, it would make good fodder for the newspapers. But I couldn't verify it, because it might be just another one of those trade rumors that are always popping up. I compromised by telling the man to call me back in fifteen minutes.

I called Bill Walker, but he wasn't around. I finally got in touch with his chauffeur, who told me that the deal had indeed been made. I was furious that I hadn't been consulted, and every time in the next several years when Camilli smashed a homer for the Phillies or the Dodgers, I muttered to myself that Bill Walker should have stayed in the fish business. This had to be one of our worst deals. Hurst played about fifty games for us that year, hitting .199.

Adding to my unhappiness, Klein was only ordinary for us. It developed that he couldn't hit lefties. Obviously, too, he felt the pressure of being with a contender.

He hit .301. Babe Herman came up with a good .304, knocking in eighty-four runs.

After 1934, Phil Wrigley decided to move in as president, and he introduced a stranger, Charles (Boots) Weber, as the front office boss. I got along very well with Boots, a personable fellow. We were still not in the baseball business as it's known now, with executives all over the place and scouts covering every area, no matter how remote, where the game is played. Our two top sleuths were Clarence (Pants) Rowland and Jack Doyle. Rowland, after a long career in the Minors, had managed the White Sox to a pennant and World Series victory over the Giants in 1917. Doyle was one of the last of the old Orioles, that hardy group, including John McGraw, that put Baltimore on the baseball map.

The Cubs we put together in 1935, who won one hundred games to take the pennant, were the best group I ever managed, even though one of the Chicago writers didn't think so when we started this most auspicious season.

This was Ralph Cannon, a hard-working and somewhat humorless man who was telling the readers of the *Daily News* about us. Every time he saw me in spring training and in the early weeks of the race he would call me "Major." I figured this was quite a compliment. I would snap my heels together and come up with a smart salute. Great public relations, I thought. This went on and on. I kept saluting and clicking my heels until one day curiosity got the better of me. I asked Ralph why he kept calling me "Major."

"Your boys remind me of those amateurs Major Bowes has on his radio program," said Ralph. Despite his inherent pessimism, Cannon was an able, conscientious reporter, even though he was slightly off base in his early assessment of my 1935 boys.

Early in the season I had taken myself off the active list after going something like forty times up without a hit in spring training. The job was Cavarretta's. During the season I went to bat only eight times and made no hits.

We almost had to crack that magic one hundred to take the pennant because the Cardinals won ninety-six and the Giants ninety-one. And, to win it, we roared down the stretch with twenty-one in a row. In all my fifty years in baseball I never experienced a season to come close to 1935. Before it started, we again had dipped into the player market and this one was to pay off handsomely.

The Cubs hadn't possessed a really top-notch lefty since Jim (Hippo) Vaughn. We found our answer with the Pirates in a deal that put us over the top. We took Larry French, a stylish southpaw, and Fred Lindstrom, the one-time boy wonder infielder of the Giants, from Pittsburgh. In return, we gave up Guy Bush, Babe Herman, and Jim Weaver, a giant right-hander.

Cub oldtimers and the come-latelies, too, may want to get a rundown on this most gifted 1935 championship club. It was Cavarretta at first, Herman at second, Jurges at short, and Hack at third in the infield. The regular outfield had Augie Galan in left, Fred Lindstrom in center, and Frank Demaree in right. Klein occasionally played in right. And George (Tuck) Stainback was another spare outfielder. Hartnett was in 116 games, hitting a lusty .344. Our pitchers were Lon Warneke, Bill Lee, Larry French, Charley Root, and Tex Carleton. Back of them were Hugh Casey, a great reliever, Roy Henshaw, Fabian Kowalik, and Clyde Shoun.

More than thirty years later, I have sharp memories

of some of these players, and I still see them in the vigor of their youth. There was, for instance, Henshaw, a little southpaw from the University of Chicago. He had fantastic success against the Pirates. He also badly outpointed me in the conversational league. His teammates called him the Professor and the name really fit. Once I inquired about a pitch he had made that had hurt us considerably.

In a very dignified manner he looked me in the eye and said: "The pitch bisected the plate."

Bill Jurges didn't know how to say good morning or good night. It wasn't that he was antisocial. I'll always think he continually thought baseball off the field, too, and just couldn't relax. And Billy Herman jollied him along. Herman was one of the finest second basemen I've seen. He could really slap the ball into right field on the hit and run. And what a glove! He normally made a play you seldom see these days—fielding a ground ball and instead of tossing to first base throwing to third, nipping the runner who had broken from second base.

French had a tremendous screwball and fine control. He was smart out there.

When we played the Braves we knew all we had to do was start Carleton, a skinny right-hander. Casey was the ideal relief pitcher with a fast ball, good control, and a lot of moxie.

Root would stick out his chin and battle you. That's why we called him Chinski. That recalls a story that goes far back before this 1935 season. Root and Adolfo Luque of the Reds were engaging in a "dusting" match in Cincy, keeping the batters jumping back for dear life.

Luque was clever. He'd break in a curve ball at the knee on a lefty batter. His battery mate was Ernie Lombardi, a gentle giant. Someone on our bench wondered aloud if Ernie was calling those dusters.

"We'll find out," said Root.

Lombardi was up and Root hit him on the elbow with his first pitch. He walked down toward first base rubbing the sore spot.

"Imagine Charley pitching that way to me," said the unsuspecting Lombardi. "Doesn't he know I like pitches on the inside!"

Warneke became an outstanding pitcher because of great effort and listening closely to Grover Cleveland Alexander, the old master. When he joined us in Catalina he couldn't field and he was wild. Give old Alex a big assist.

Cavarretta, of course, was a natural, doing everything. Stan Hack was a smooth, relaxed ball player, a good pinch hitter, and was always heads up. Augie (Goo Goo) Galan found himself in the outfield after an erratic season at second base, and he gave everything he had.

The enigma on our club was Tuck Stainback. I still wonder why he didn't become one of the best. He had a great arm, he could run, and he had a good swing. Before he came up to us from the Pacific Coast League he had been beaned by Roy Joiner. Maybe that hurt him.

Lindstrom was a vital asset. He started the 1935 season at third base, ahead of Hack. But we were hurting for a center fielder. We knew Lindstrom had played it with the Pirates the two previous seasons, between the Waner brothers, Paul and Lloyd. Hard Rock Johnson gave Fred a fungo workout and came to me. "You've got a center fielder right here on the club," he said. So it was Fred in center. More than that, Lindstrom became the boss of the outfield. With his great experience, he cleverly positioned his two associates so well that only seven pop flies fell safely during that twenty-one game streak.

Lindstrom drove in the winning run, or scored it, in seven of those games during this most spectacular Cub streak of all time. The happy day was September 27 in old Sportsman's Park in St. Louis. The Cardinals, who had beaten the Tigers in the 1934 World Series, were still in the race, but if we could beat Dizzy Dean in the first game of a doubleheader the pennant was ours. The Cardinals broke in front with two runs in the first inning, but it wasn't all Bill Lee's fault. Billy Herman and Stan Hack made errors, but the damage was held to two runs when Lindstrom threw out a runner at the plate. But Diz on this day wasn't the great pitcher you've read about. The Cubs flogged him for fifteen hits, Lindstrom getting three singles and a double, driving in three runs in a 6 to 2 victory, Lee's twentieth of the year. It eliminated the Cardinals, who finished second, four games behind.

Frankie Frisch had ordered Dean to pitch inside to Lindstrom. But Fred, whose style was to move into the pitch, pulled away on old Diz, foiling his "jamming" technique. After Fred's third hit, Frisch yelled to Dean: "You dumb so-and-so, pitch him inside!"

"I AM pitching him inside," Dean hollered.

We made it twenty-one in a row in the second game by beating Mike Ryba, 5 to 3. Again, we had to rally. A three-run burst in the seventh tied it and two in the ninth won it. Roy Henshaw, who had replaced Root, was the winner.

There are always freakish things surrounding a streak. At the start of this remarkable success string, a rotund lad named Paul Dominick had showed up in a Cub uniform. I never knew where he came from, but this fifteen-year-old boy was welcome as a good luck charm.

The day this twenty-one-game fling got into motion, I noticed a hammer and some tacks on the bench. I picked up the hammer and drove a tack into my right shoe. The next day I repeated the act. The 22nd tack had no magic, but who cared then?

After that double victory in St. Louis, we didn't waste any time getting to the Chase Hotel and the victory celebration Bob Lewis was arranging. Woody English brought his scissors along and snipped off every tie in sight, including Phil Wrigley's. I batted out a few tunes on the banjo. There was no shortage of wet goods, but I have no memory of champagne. Correct me if I'm wrong, but I think we settled for bourbon and scotch.

We were confident we would bring the Cubs their first world title since 1908, when they had whipped the Tigers four out of five. Once again, the Tigers were our opponents. Led by Mickey Cochrane, they had beaten out the Yankees. Cochrane's Tigers had lost to the Cardinals in the 1934 showdown in seven games. And in this year, Henry Ford signed a four-year contract at $100,000 per annum for the radio broadcasting rights! It was to be a memorable and somewhat messy series.

The series opened in Detroit. Warneke held the Tigers to four hits and won, 4 to 0. But the next day the Tigers clobbered Root for four runs in a first inning knockout and won, 6 to 3, behind Tommy Bridges, a little curveball expert. The competition moved to Chicago, setting up one of the most heated games in World Series competition. Both clubs had great bench jockeys, and I'll be the last one to deny that the great Hank Greenberg was our main target. Do you heckle a substitute or a star? And, in that third game, Hank went out with a broken arm in a collision at the plate.

We thought that it all started in Detroit when Hank turned his venom on Cavarretta. So we retaliated. George Moriarty, one of the umpires and a former Tiger who had managed that club, came up with a stern warning.

The third game was a sizzler before the Tigers won in the eleventh, 6 to 5. There was a close play at second base, and I rushed out to challenge Moriarty's decision.

He chased me. But the Cub bench continued broadcasting. Moriarty shagged Woody English and Tuck Stainback. All this time, I stood in the dark runway back of our dugout and directed through a hole I'd punched in the door. Bill Lee started the game against Elden Auker, a submarine right-hander, but was knocked out in the eighth inning when the Tigers scored four times to go ahead 5 to 3. We tied it in the ninth when Jurges and Klein delivered as pinch batters, but the Tigers beat French in the eleventh.

The upshot of this wild game was that Herman, Jurges, English, myself, and Umpire Moriarty were fined $200 each after the series ended. The basis was naughty language. Moriarty had no complaints. His strong language had been heard by both Commissioner Landis and Ford Frick, the National League president. These were the heaviest fines ever levied in a World Series. And Jurges still was jawing with Moriarty to the finish. It's on the record that I paid the fines levied against English, Jurges, and Herman.

Detroit made it three in a row the next day. Alvin Crowder beat Carleton, 2 to 1. Our only run came in the second, when Hartnett hit a homer. We prolonged the series the next afternoon when Warneke, with help from Lee, beat Schoolboy Rowe, 3 to 1. A muscle injury forced Lon to leave in the sixth and his arm was never quite the same after that.

The series returned to Detroit, and it was French against Bridges. We went into the ninth with the score tied, 3 to 3. Hack led off with a triple. Jurges, eighth in the batting order, was up. A hit, a roller to the infield, or a fly ball would break the deadlock. But Jurges fanned.

Next up was French. A pinch batter? I considered it. But Larry was pitching very well. Lefty hitters would be coming up for the Tigers. I decided to keep Larry in the game. He tapped back to Bridges and was thrown out. Hack, representing that big run, still was on third base. The opportunity was over when Galan flied out.

Flea Clifton, a right-hand hitter, was retired at the start of the Tigers' ninth. The next three swung from the left side and that's the big reason I had kept French in the game. But Cochrane singled and moved to second base when Charley Gehringer, another lefty, grounded out. This brought up Goose Goslin, who also swung from the left side. He didn't hit the ball well, but it dropped in short center for the hit that beat us. This was the Tigers' first World Series victory. Sad to relate it, it was the Cubs' fifth successive defeat in the glitter show.

Yes, I later second-guessed myself for not sending up a batter for French in that ninth inning. But, who knows, French might have dribbled a run-scoring roller. I still think I was right. Our other pitchers were pretty well used up or ineffective.

I was alone with my thoughts the next night in Chicago, still asking myself if I had goofed. I decided I would not show myself at any of the more popular Near North Side spots, choosing a cozy little chop-suey joint where I was sure no one would recognize the Cub manager who had blown the World Series.

I sat there quietly and the man came up to take my order. The Chinaman looked me over.

"You Jolly Cholly Grimm?" he inquired.

I pleaded guilty, still confident he wouldn't know what had happened in Detroit.

"How come you don't get Hack in from third base?" he inquired, most resolutely.

If that place is still in business, I'm sure my chop suey dish is still setting there!

Our biggest change for 1936 was sending Klein back to the Phillies for Curt Davis, who had been an exceptional right-hander with a poor ball club. Curt, beset by aches and pains, wasn't to help us much with an 11–9 record. But we were in the race until late August, when the Giants put on a spurt. The Cubs wound up in a second-place tie with the Cardinals. This was my last playing year. I batted 132 times, hitting .250. What I'm most proud of is the fact that I had 297 putouts and thirty-three assists without an error.

It wasn't until early in January of 1937 that I signed for another year as manager. There had been some unfounded rumors that I was on the way out and that Phil Wrigley would be vacating the president's chair. But he reelected himself, a privilege that goes along with owning 80 percent of the stock.

We figured more punch was needed for 1937, and we sacrificed Warneke to get Jim (Rip) Collins from the Cardinals. This would free Cavarretta for the outfield, with Collins playing first base. Rip, in addition to being a fine ball player, was a great conversationalist and he'd talk to the rival players as he rounded the bases, but would never say anything that made them mad. Once he told me, "Keep trying, kid. Some day you'll be as good a first baseman as me!" Rip had taken over from a pretty good first baseman in St. Louis—Sunny Jim Bottomley. He fitted into that Cardinal Gas House picture and a little of his spirit rubbed off on us during his two years in Wrigley Field.

We traded Woody English to the Dodgers after the 1936 season, coming up with Linus Frey. With Woody gone, Hartnett became the team captain.

Back trouble felled me in Boston in mid-July of 1937. The doctors never could pinpoint my trouble, but I think it goes back to my first year with the Cubs when I collided with Jack Scott, a pitcher, in a play at first base. So there I was in my hotel suite in the old Somerset Hotel, doubled up with pain and waited on hand and foot by faithful Bob Lewis. I have this old *Tribune* clipping that gives a play-by-play of my distress:

The scene in Grimm's room tonight was amusing. He laughs about the electric cords hanging from the ceiling and leading under the covers of his bed. Every once in a while he gulps either a red, white, or purple pill. At the bottom of the doctor's chart he scribbled: "If still alive tomorrow morning, take whatever remains, regardless of color."

Between phone calls, Traveling Secretary Lewis, who has volunteered as a nurse, rushes up to his bedside and yells that it's time for another pill. Lewis doesn't worry about the color of them. Neither does Grimm. He takes the first one within reach.

After the game, a newspaper photographer asked Charlie to close his eyes. Grimm kicked off the covers and yelled: "Get outta here! I'm not dead yet!"

When Grimm left the hotel to take a train for St. Louis for examination by Dr. Robert Hyland, it was a most unusual scene. Back Bay station is only two or three blocks away, so Charlie made the trip in a wheel chair. Leading the procession was Lewis. Pushing the chair was a uniformed hotel porter. Grimm sat upright in his chair, holding his cane like a scepter and bowing like a politician or monarch to spectators along the line of march. Bringing up the rear was Trainer Andy Lotshaw, whose bowed head and sober mien indicated he had been hired out as the chief mourner.

Hartnett took over for the few days I needed to get back on my feet. Other Cubs had troubles, too. Bill Lee was ailing in August from a pulled muscle in his side that kept him idle for two weeks. That same month, Rip Collins suffered an ankle fracture.

Late in August we went into a month-long slump that wiped out a seven-game lead and tumbled us into second place. This brought the tavern masterminds and even some of the reporters into action. But early in September, Phil Wrigley flew to New York and set the rumors at rest, giving me a contract for 1938. We finished second, two games behind the Giants.

Out on Catalina Island, in the early days of spring training for 1938, I went into a huddle with Hartnett and Clarence Rowland, the all-purpose baseball man who then was a top scout for us. We knew that Dizzy Dean had lost his fast ball, but Gabby and I were confident he could help us. Later we met with Phil Wrigley and Hartnett pointed out that Dean would be a "stop" pitcher. Phil wanted to know what that meant and Gabby explained a "stopper" is one who can be depended on to win the big games and to bust a losing streak.

"Dean's the man the boys want. Let's go get him!" Wrigley told Rowland.

Clarence caught up with the touring Cardinals in Springfield, Missouri, just before the season opened. "I rode with them back to St. Louis," Rowland later reported. "I was the house guest of Branch Rickey and the result was a $300,000 deal. I called Mr. Wrigley in Chicago from St. Louis and told him the deal had been made. 'That's fine,' he said. 'Now I can go back to California.'"

To get old Diz, we gave $185,000 in cash, plus pitchers Curt Davis and Clyde Shoun, and Tuck Stainback. It was a good deal for us and we actually came out ahead financially. Diz was a tremendous drawing card, not only in Wrigley Field, but in the other parks. He was to win seven and lose only one for us, a vital contribution to the League title.

Dean was a great guy on a ball club and he had friends in every city, but he never took any of the players with him. He was a mischievous, boyish guy—and what a pitcher, even after that fast ball was gone!

Sometimes he'd take a few steps toward the plate and talk to the batter. I always thought he "looked" a lot of guys out. They tell me that during the 1934 World Series against the Tigers, he'd stroll past the Detroit dugout and make a point of asking Hank Greenberg if he was in the lineup. After a "yes" by the slugger, Dizzy would point his finger at him and say: "I'm going to strike you out every time you come up."

This was a trick of those old Gas Housers from St. Louis. They would pick on players who might get flustered and start pressing. When Diz came to us he said, "I'm going to make them hit the ball." His hard one still was good enough to make his slow stuff effective, but he no longer was a strikeout pitcher. He fought you out there to the last pitch and never lost confidence. To the end he had a good curve and great control. He worked hard that spring of 1938, but he no longer had the arm to pitch regularly. Even so, he often grabbed a ball during the season and headed for the bullpen, inviting a call to help out.

I remember the time we were having a clubhouse meeting when Diz still was with the Cardinals. The discussion came down on how to pitch to Pepper Martin.

"Don't throw him anything out and away," Hartnett told Malone, the pitcher of the afternoon.

A guy jumped up in the back of the room and ex-claimed, "Oh, my God, don't pitch like that to Pepper. He'll murder you!"

It was Dizzy, who had come from across the hall to sit in on the meeting.

With the exception of Dean and Tony Lazzeri, whom we picked up from the Yankees, this was just about the same team from 1937. Tony didn't play much. I was deter-mined that we'd win in 1938, and when we didn't start moving, I began to fret.

I had always sat with the players in the clubhouse and tried to be one of them. But in this season of 1938, some-thing happened to me. It's still a mystery. I brooded. I sat in front of the locker with my head in my hands. I real-ized my state of mind was hurting the Cubs. I told Phil this when we met in mid-July. He was sympathetic, and I was grateful when he asked me to suggest the man who should take over. I recommended Hartnett, then thirty-seven and in his seventeenth season as a Cub.

I left that night for my farm near St. Louis, convinced my Cub career was over. But I underestimated the esteem Phil held for me and perhaps my own luck in bouncing back.

Darned if I didn't immediately go into radio, teaming up with Pat Flanagan for the remainder of the season. We worked both the Cub and White Sox games. We were in the booth and I was jawing away at the mike that twi-light evening when Hartnett hit the homer that turned the pennant tide for the Cubs.

If any catcher had a greater arm than Gabby, I must have been looking the other way. He threw it hard, he threw it accurately—and it came in like a feather. Some players throw a ball that arrives like a piece of lead, but

Natives welcome Gabby Hartnett and Ray Campbell to spring training on Catalina Island. (Photo courtesy of the National Baseball Library, Cooperstown, New York)

Gabby's floated in gently to the shortstop or second baseman.

When Gabby was catching, there were two umpires back of the plate. He could give the man in blue a pretty good going over when he thought he had booted one. But he'd do it without turning around, and the fans never suspected it. Gabby was uncanny on high popups along the line and back of the plate. I believe he dropped only one popper in his nineteen years of wearing the harness for the Cubs.

As my successor, Hartnett untied the knots in the Cubs after I had failed. We were fourth on the rainy day he took over, five and one-half games behind the Pirates. But the Cubs didn't get any better immediately. In fact, they were eight behind at the end of July. And on August 20 they were still eight games behind, eliminating most pennant thoughts. Both the Pirates and Giants were hot. On September 4, the Cubs trailed by seven. Then they started flying, gaining ground by beating both the Giants and Pirates. On September 23 they beat the Phillies twice, moving to within two games of the top.

The Pirates, leading by a game and a half, came into Wrigley Field on September 27. Dean won it, 2 to 1, with ninth-inning help from Bill Lee. The next day the Cubs came up in the ninth with the score tied. It was evident that, with darkness closing in, this would be the final inning. Mace Brown had two out and two strikes on Gabby. The rest is history. It was a homer, and the Cubs were on their way to a pennant. When I saw that the ball was on its way over the left-field wall, I fell off my chair in the WBBM booth. I don't know what happened to my partner, Flanagan, but I do know that I finished the broadcast sitting on the floor.

But once again, the Yankees and my old friend Joe

McCarthy made it four straight over the Cubs in the
World Series.[1]

Once again decline followed defeat in the World Series. Gabby's magic moment had no sequel. After finishing fourth in 1939 and fifth in 1940, Hartnett was removed in favor of veteran catcher Jimmy Wilson who
had managed the Phillies for a few years. Cub general
manager Boots Weber returned to California and sportswriter James T. Gallagher assumed the non-enviable
task of finding some players for Wilson to manage.

When Gallagher sent old heroes like Billy Herman
and Larry French to the Brooklyn Dodgers, later to be
joined by Augie Galan, and when that trio helped the
Dodgers to the 1941 pennant, Gallagher became the
whipping boy of Chicago press and fans.

The Cubs of 1941–43 were sixth, sixth and fifth and
it was no surprise when Wilson was fired when the 1944
Cubs lost 10 in a row after an opening day win. Charlie
Grimm, who with Bill Veeck had been running the Milwaukee Brewers travelling baseball show, came back
again to lead the Cubs.

Charlie said later that taking that team from last to
fourth place was the best managing job he ever did. But
he did a great job in 1945 too. **Here is his account of
that monumental year:**

We did most of our training indoors for the 1945 season, which ended a run of three straight pennants for
Billy Southworth and the Cardinals. They had romped
in 1944 with 105 victories. Because of the war-time travel
restrictions, we worked out in French Lick, Indiana.
Our headquarters was the West Baden Hotel, and it was

fortunate for us that the ballroom was huge enough for exercising purposes. It was one of the wettest springs in my memory, and I don't think we worked outdoors more than three or four times. This was an old ballclub and the players benefited from the mineral baths there.

Phil Cavarretta, whom I had made captain of the team, was tremendous. He won the batting title with a .355 and was voted the most valuable player in the National League. We took the lead on July 8 and were never headed, winning 98 games, divided right down the middle at home and away. One of the major reasons we beat out the Cardinals by three games was our 21–1 record against the Reds.

The most spectacular deal of the 1945 season was for Hank Borowy. All baseball and the newspaper reporters were puzzled when Hank changed uniforms. He had been a Yankee star, but now, on July twenty-seventh, he was hustled off to a contender in the other League.

For the Cubs to make a bid for Borowy, he first would have to be waived out of the American League, or, in simpler language, passed up by the other seven clubs, which could claim him for a few thousand dollars on waivers. Almost every player, including the great stars, has been on a waiver list. The catch is that the waivers can be withdrawn. A team seeing a Joe DiMaggio or a Ron Santo on the waiver list would naturally assume that if a claim were made, it would be refused. Apparently, this is what happened in the Borowy case. The other American League clubs didn't even bother to put in a bid for him, figuring it would be a wasted effort. Now Larry MacPhail, who perhaps needed some cash and was disenchanted with Hank to boot, could invite the Cubs to make an offer. They did, and they got him.

"It is reasonable to estimate that this is a $100,000

deal in players and cash," said MacPhail. It's hard to believe that this was less than a quarter of a century ago and that now a high-school phenom will command that much money before he has ever worn a uniform with the pros.

"Borowy appears to have outlived his usefulness with the Yankees. Since April he has pitched only four complete games and appears to have outlived his usefulness to us," continued Larry. A few years before, when Larry was with the Brooklyn Dodgers, he had made a slick deal with the Cubs for Billy Herman. I've often thought he showed his appreciation by clearing the way for us to land Borowy, without whom we never would have won that 1945 pennant.

Yes, we needed a Borowy, or an Alexander or a Johnson. Neither could have helped us more than did Hank. He had won ten and lost five with the Yankees. With the Cubs, he was sensational. Scarcely more than two months were left in the season, but Hank won for us eleven times against two defeats. Hank, an overhanded pitcher, had a good fast ball, a matching curve, and a fine change of pace, which kept the batters off balance. I soon learned that the reason he'd failed to finish many games with the Yankees was because he suffered from a blister on his second finger from the seams on the ball. Andy Lotshaw did a wonderful job keeping this busted skin under control.

Hank, who gave out with all his might on every pitch, was our only pitcher who could hold his own with the Cardinals, who beat us sixteen times in twenty-two games in 1945. I wonder if a pennant winner ever was outpointed that badly by one of its rivals? Hank beat the Cardinals three out of four and his only loss was a 1 to 0 heartbreaker to Harry (The Cat) Brecheen.

I don't mean to go overboard on Borowy. In seventy-four of our ninety-eight victories I never called on a relief pitcher. This figure couldn't be matched today if a manager had four starters of the caliber of Ed Walsh, Walter Johnson, Lefty Grove, and Sandy Koufax. The bullpen has grown that important. Hank Wyse won twenty-two games, all but one of them complete efforts! Claude Passeau and Paul Derringer each went the distance fourteen times. Borowy, Ray Prim, Hy Vandenberg, Bob Chipman, and Paul Erickson helped swell the total.

When Borowy came to us as a beautiful present he had won 46 and lost 25 in three and a half seasons with the Yankees. He stayed with us three more seasons, but never approached his fantastic showing of 1945. Thereafter he was 25–32 with us and drifted out of the limelight. But I'm willing to cast a vote for him as the all-time sudden Cub!

At any rate, the Cubs and Tigers were going to meet each other in the World Series for the fourth time since 1907.

Both teams, because of the war-time shortage of talent, obviously were below par. Perhaps Warren Brown said it best. When he was being polled by a wire service for his prediction, Warren said: "I don't think either team can win it."

Well, it wasn't quite that bad, though the play at times was not up to World Series standards. We lost it in seven games, but I'll always think we would have brought the Wrigleys their first world championship had not Passeau suffered a torn nail on the middle finger of his pitching hand in the sixth inning of the sixth game. The injury came on a drive by Jimmy Outlaw. At the end of the sixth inning we were ahead, 5 to 1, having knocked out Virgil Trucks in a four-run fifth. Passeau had to leave in the seventh when the Tigers scored twice. The Tigers tied it with four in the eighth and I had to call on Borowy, who had pitched five innings the day before. Hank blanked the Tigers for four innings and we won in the twelfth, 8 to 7, on a freakish play.

With one out in the twelfth, Frank Secory batted for Len Merullo and singled to center off Dizzy Trout. Bill Schuster ran for Secory, and a minute later we had the series tied. Hack hit safetly to left, and when the ball bounced over Hank Greenberg's head, Schuster scored. It first was ruled as a single, plus an error for Greenberg. A few hours later, the official scorers, given evidence that the ball had hit a drain plug in the outfield, called it a double.

After a day's pause in the series, I sent Borowy against the Tigers in the deciding game. He was now coming into his fourth game of the series, the third in succession, but he was our hot pitcher and I figured he was our best bet, especially because Passeau had been knocked out of action by that line drive. Claude, I'm sure, could have won that decisive game for us had he been fit.

Passeau had blanked the Tigers, 3 to 0, on one hit in the third game after the teams had divided the first two. Borowy opened with a 9 to 0 shutout triumph against Hal Newhouser. Trucks beat Hank Wyse in the second game, 4 to 1. In his great performance, Passeau yielded a single to Rudy York in the second and walked Bill Swift at the start of the sixth. These were the only Detroit base runners.

The Tigers evened the series when it moved to Wrigley Field, Trout beating our lefty, Ray Prim, 4 to 1. Ray was a thirty-nine-year-old southpaw and after he had retired the first nine, he ran into a four-run burst in the fourth.

It was Borowy vs. Newhouser in the fifth game, but this time the result was reversed. The Tigers scored once in the third inning but might have made more had not Pafko made great catches of drives by Doc Cramer and Greenberg. The Tigers scored four times in the sixth against Borowy and Hy Vandenberg. Newhouser had won twenty-five during the season. He was a great one.

We had to win the sixth game to keep the series alive. It started out with Passeau matched against Trucks. The Cubs came into the fifth trailing by a run, but knocked out the Tiger flame-thrower with a four-run barrage. Hack and Cavarretta each delivered two-run singles. Greenberg hit a homer off Prim for the last of four runs, which tied the score in the eighth. Then we won it in the twelfth.

While I had great confidence in Borowy, I don't think I waited too long to take him out in that seventh game. The first three singled, Hank made only nine pitches. Next, I called on Paul Derringer. He walked in a runner before Paul Richards cleared the bases with a double for a five-run inning. I used four other pitchers, including Passeau, who was bumped for two runs in the eighth. We wound up losing the game, 9 to 3, along with the series. I felt bad. All losers do. But it couldn't take away the fact that in our season we had unseated the mighty Cardinals.[2]

The third-place finish by the Cubs in 1946 was the last time they would see the first division for 21 years! While other clubs were loaded with players returning from the war and had talented youngsters being readied in their farm systems, the Cubs clung too long to their over-the-hill gang and neglected to tend the farm. Still, finishing in the basement in 1948 was a real shock to P. K. Wrigley and even though Gallagher proclaimed that "the 1948

Cubs were the best team ever to finish last," Mr. Wrigley placed an ad in the Chicago papers:

To Chicago Cub Fans

The Cub management wants you to know we appreciate the wonderful support you are giving the ball club. We want you fans and Charlie Grimm to have a team that can be up at the top—the kind of team that both of you deserve.

We also know that this year's rebuilding job has been a flop. But we are not content—and never have been—to just go along with an eye on attendance only. We want a winner, just as you do, and we will do everything possible to get one.

If one system does not work, we will try another. Your loyal support when we are down is a real incentive for us to try even harder to do everything in our power to give us all a winner.

Thanks,
The Chicago Cubs

By June of the following season, Grimm was out as manager, succeeded by fiery Frankie Frisch, whose fighting spirit was seen as the right medicine for the lackluster Cubs.

About this time, Mr. Wrigley wondered aloud what had happened to the two million dollars he had invested in trying to find, develop and buy talent since 1946. Well, $100,000 went to the Dodgers for Preston Ward and Paul Minner, $35,000 to the Braves for Bill Voiselle, etc., etc.

Early in 1950, Gallagher was shifted to other duties so that a new director of player personnel could be appointed. He was Branch Rickey's understudy at Brooklyn and his name was Wid Matthews.

— 5 —

GOING DOWN

If nostalgia buffs can look back on the fifties as fabulous, Cub fans simply cannot. The period, 1948–1967, was their dark night of the soul, their long march, the time that tried their heart and patience. During this period a new breed of Cub fan was forged. These Cub fans were not the kind who could applaud when Joe McCarthy, the greatest manager of his time, was fired for losing a World Series. These Cub fans lived without the luxury of winning a pennant every three years. These Cub fans not only had to endure countless beatings over endless seasons of mediocrity, they had to hear the perennial proclamation that success was one trade, one rookie, one year away. It was the era of Wid Matthews and later the College of Coaches; it was the time when Bert Wilson, Jack Quinlan, Jack Brickhouse, Vince Lloyd, Lou Boudreau and others reminded the fans that Wrigley Field was still majestic in its beauty even if what happened on the field was less than lovely.

Spring training in 1950 was preceded by a party and some promises. **Edgar Munzel described the scene:**

> Gratitude is traditionally not listed among the shining virtues of most baseball players. But you will never convince Owner P. K. Wrigley of that insofar as his 1950 Chicago Cubs are concerned.

Wrigley, who had tossed a $7,000 "get-acquainted" party for the Cubs in a ten-day pre-training session at Catalina Island, was the grand host once again just before the team broke camp and set sail for the mainland. He entertained the entire squad, plus wives, at an all-day outing that included a 35-mile tour of the island, a calf-roping exhibition and a steak barbecue.

But the high spot came when Capt. Phil Cavarretta assembled the squad and then called Mr. Wrigley. With the Cubs clustered in a semi-circle around him, Cavarretta presented the owner with a pocket watch, saying:

"This is just a little token of our appreciation of all you have done for us here this spring. And we hope that we can give you an even better present by winning a few ball games for you this year."

Wrigley, always poised and at ease, was so deeply moved he could only stammer his thanks. He quickly retreated and showed the watch to his wife. It was engraved: "In appreciation of the splendid vacation you gave the 1950 Chicago Cubs."

Mrs. Wrigley looked at the watch and broke into tears. Later she remarked: "You know, Phil does so much for other people, but that's the first time anybody ever has given him anything."[1]

Captain Cavarretta was right: The Cubs did win a few and it was a splendid vacation.

Frankie Frisch, the old Fordham Flash, had the likes of Terwilliger, Ward, Sauer, Pafko, Serena, Smalley and Mickey Owen playing near .500 for the first half of the season. But by August they had fallen apart and landed in seventh place. But for a few additions over the winter,

Wid wanted to stand pat. As May of 1951 ended, the Cubs were within a few games of first. Then came one of the patented June swoons. Matthews made "the deal that defies the laws of sanity" and sent Andy Pafko and three others to Brooklyn for four lesser lights. The sportswriters had a field day berating Wid. A month later, dissension on the team reached the boiling point and the Old Flash was sent packing. Some of the columns in the Chicago papers are worth reprinting:

PLAYERS BLAST FRISCH
by Neil R. Gazel

PHILADELPHIA—The Cubs might have climbed into National League flag contention this season, but for one drawback: player morale has sunk lower than a dry well. More than half the team is antagonistic to Manager Frank Frisch and his frantic exhortations. "He doesn't know what he's doing," several players have asserted, "he's worse than last season."

"You know what the trouble is," commented one spokesman, "but you can't do anything . . . or say anything."

"He's let the newspapermen run the club," volunteered another.

"Frisch is the lousiest, blankety-blank manager in baseball," was another comment.

"Nobody can do anything right."

It is not the purpose here to pass judgment on Frisch. As he points out himself: "When you lose, you're called a lousy manager; you're great when you win."[2]

On July 21, 1951 in Philadelphia, Frisch was fired and, in a sense, so was his successor, Phil Cavarretta. P. K.

Not even fiery Frankie Frisch could inspire the Cubs of the early
'50s.

Wrigley let it be known that Phil would only finish out
the season at the helm. **Warren Brown summed up the
situation:**

There's one thing certain about the Chicago Cubs.
They keep one in practice on the hail and farewell
technique.

Seems like only yesterday the boys were busy on
the story of Frank Frisch, who had succeeded Charlie Grimm, who had succeeded Jimmy Wilson, who
had succeeded Gabby Hartnett, who had succeeded
Charlie Grimm, etc., etc., etc. And now the life story
of Phil Cavarretta is in the mill.

If P. K. Wrigley has been quoted correctly in the
dispatches from Lake Geneva, Cavarretta is merely
doing a John Corriden and finishing out the season. Thus Phil would seem to be taking over with
two strikes on him. I'd worry more about that were
it not for the fact that I have to go very far back in
Cub history to come up with a manager who didn't
have two strikes on him when he took the job.

My personal wish is that Phil will be the Cub
manager as long as he has been a Cub player, if only
to give the boys surcease from writing the life story
of the next one.

That the familiar Cub managerial award known
as the Gate was given to Frank Frisch was not
surprising.

Nor was it surprising that the award of the Gate
was made in Philadelphia. If you're a follower of
past performances you'd have to pick that city, for
there it was that the Old Flash enjoyed some of his
greatest moments in establishing that he did not
have any longer the temperamental balance needed

to handle the delicate sensibilities of the modern Cubs.[3]

Though the Cubs came in last, Cavarretta was kept as manager for the 1952 season. As early as January, Wid Matthews was already crowing about the great season coming up. **Davis J. Walsh of the *Daily News* recorded the event:**

The scene was a private dining room in the Wrigley Restaurant, just across the big "moat" on Michigan av. The time, yesterday noon. The occasion, uncertain.

It might have been a testimonial luncheon for manager Phil Cavarretta, "Chicago's own." It could have been a prearranged meeting of the minds (sic) between the press and radio on one side and the Chicago National League baseball club on the other.

We never did find out about that, because the seating arrangements seemed just a little haphazard and confusing. They left some of the guests giving one another the back of the neck, so to say. And, at the same time, facing others with the affect of rival squads, drawn up across the line of scrimmage.

Meantime, the Messrs. Cavarretta and Wid Matthews were down at one end, facing everybody and with their backs to the wall, which seemed fair enough. That's where they were the last time we looked, back in early October.

Seated halfway up along the left flank, with an air of grave detachment, was Philip K. Wrigley, who owns the restaurant, the building, the ball club and his chewing-gum empire.

Personnel Director Matthews, in calling the occasion to order, made no reference to Cavarretta (seated on his immediate left), but instead announced that "Mr. Wrigley's patience" (with a last-place club) was at an end. That being a new "party line" on the North Side, everybody looked at Mr. Wrigley.

Mr. Wrigley continued to look noncommittal. In fact, very.

While Matthews went on to develop this particular theme, publicity director Cliff Jaffe passed around data, bearing on and appertaining to Cub training-trip personnel for 1952—which seemed unfortunate.

Anyhow, it revealed that the most promising ball player on the Cub roster was 35-year-old Phil Cavarretta, the manager, since his .311 of last year was the only proven evidence of an ability to hit major league pitching.

Of course there were Dee Fondy's .374 and catcher Harry Chiti's .301 but these were made, respectively, at Los Angeles and Des Moines. For the most part, the others apparently couldn't be relied upon to hit an audible foul. . . .

"Of course," Mr. Matthews was saying in answer to a question, "if we're going to dream, let's dream good ones."

From halfway up along the left flank came a polite objection, "Let's not dream at all. We've had too much of that already" . . . It seemed to be the rich, full baritone of Philip K. Wrigley.

Cavarretta sat quietly watchful throughout, but spoke incisively when asked a direct question. Yes, he might play as many as 80 games at first base, provided Fondy didn't prove himself a better man for the job. Having said this, he stopped abruptly and waited for more.

Yes, it was true that the Cubs had three or four outfielders who could hit pretty well and, on defense, "scramble" with the best of them. Said Cavarretta tersely:

"I'll take one 'scrambler' in centerfield. The other two have got to hit."

Matthews had previously said something about having offered pitcher Bob Rush to Brooklyn for either first baseman Gil Hodges or outfielder Duke Snider. Which of the two would Cavarretta prefer, if given a choice?

He said "Snider"—just like that—and didn't elaborate. He didn't need to. Mr. Wrigley said nothing with melancholy eloquence.[4]

Cavarretta, in fact, took the 1952 Cubs all the way up to fifth. Hank Sauer had an MVP season, Frankie Baumholtz hit .325 and Bob Rush and Warren Hacker posted 17 and 15 wins respectively.

Wid Matthews did his part to strengthen the team over the winter by trading Walt Dubiel to the Braves for Sheldon Jones. And when the season started slowly, he sent five players and $100,000 to his old boss Branch Rickey, now Pirate G. M., for Ralph Kiner, Joe Garagiola and two other discards. The Cub outfield with Kiner in one corner and Sauer in the other became legendary.

In September, some good looking rookies like Gene Baker, Ernie Banks and Don Elston were brought up and helped the Cubs to a 10-game winning streak. Wid was positively ecstatic. Manager Cavarretta felt somewhat more reserved. The seventh-place finish didn't exactly point to a pennant in the near future.

Seventeen of the 40 players reporting to spring training in 1954 were rookies, the products of Wid Matthews'

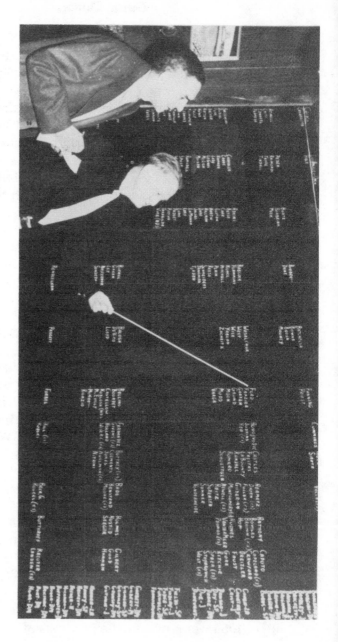

Wid Matthews, whose five-year plan turned into seven years of mediocrity.

rebuilding. Their names are legendary: John Pyecha, Bob Hartig, Chris Kitsos, Harold Meek, Bob Murray, Burdette Thurlby. . . . Gone was Roy Smalley, who was finally traded after enduring six seasons as the target of Cub fans' frustrations. Charlie Grimm recalled later how kids sitting behind the first base dugout used to bring gloves to catch Smalley's errant throws from shortstop. Smalley was a lanky guy with quickness, great range and a rag arm. He would make a truly magnificent play on one grounder and then let one go right under his glove. When told that he had been traded, he said, "I have to admit I'm relieved to be getting away from the fans at Wrigley Field." Cub fans who booed Roy are probably sorry. What they should have done in those days was have "Vegetable Day" and make the general manager circle the park so the fans could put the blame and the tomatoes where they really belonged.

As spring training unfolded, Manager Cavarretta told Mr. Wrigley the truth: the material was just not there and not even Cub fans were loyal enough to pay to see a team with no present and no apparent future. For his honesty, Cavarretta was fired! Another Cub first: no team had ever fired the manager in spring training. The press came to the fray with zingers abounding. **Witness Warren Brown's column in the** *Herald-American:*

COLUMBUS, Ga.—March 31—So Winnowing Wid Matthews has outlasted another Cub manager. Once again the most curiously conducted baseball club in the major leagues has seen fit to follow the pattern that it is much easier to get a new manager than acceptable ball players.

That Phil Cavarretta, given the option of exchanging places with Stan Hack, or else, promptly chose the or-else, should be fired is not surprising. It was common knowledge Winnowing Wid, in mid-season of 1953, wanted to get rid of the manager—an old Cub custom—but had his hand stayed because Owner P. K. Wrigley then had other ideas.

That Cavarretta should be dumped in the midst of a Spring training season would be completely baffling to anyone who didn't suspect that Winnowing Wid, long on platitudes and short on worthwhile accomplishment, didn't feel the urgent need of a smoke-screen to obscure one of his recent most embarrassing moments.

A few days ago the Brooklyn club sold Infielder Bobby Morgan to the Phillies.

Now Wid's apologists in Chicago have certainly quoted him upside down and backwards for months on end on how he had what the ex-master, Frank Leahy, would call "a burning desire" to land Morgan. But Morgan went to the Phillies. He went there even though Brooklyn's Buzz Bavasi was authority for the statement that Morgan was offered to the Cubs for Roy Smalley and a reasonable amount of cash. Matthews—advertised often as eager to make a deal—either ignored this, or turned it down.

It seems reasonable that even the apologists might have started asking pertinent questions about this. They'll not, now, of course, because the Cavarretta incident is of much more importance.

Down here in the red clay country, the news of Cavarretta's firing was restricted, at first, to a brief story.

When Frantic Frank Lane learned of it, his one comment was worth repeating:

"What could Cavarretta, or any other manager,

possibly have done to merit being fired in the middle of Spring training? If they didn't want him, why didn't they attend to this before training started?"

Later an Associated Press story on the latest of the Cubs' strange interludes quoted from all principals.

I have had reason to believe for some time that Winnowing Wid had sold himself completely to Wrigley, even though he has yet to do so with Chicago fandom, and with experienced baseball men around the country.

How complete a sales job Matthews had done I didn't realize until I read this Associated Press story.

Quotes from Wrigley at Phoenix concluded this wise:

" . . . he (Cavarretta) said he did not have the kind of ball players he wanted. He had sort of given up on the boys, feeling that they were not pennant material. Well, maybe not, but they could be with the will-to-win."

"The will-to-win," huh? right from Page One of Winnowing Wid's book of cliches.

Well, folks, if in subsequent interviews Wrigley starts talking about orientation, seeking one's proper level, and the figures are not a true estimate of this (or that) individual's true worth, stand by for the life rafts.

Needless to say, as one who has known Phil Cavarretta, man and boy, in all the years he was associated with the Cubs, I feel sorry for him. He deserved a better fate than to become a casualty of the misguided missile, Winnowing Wid Matthews, much as Wid wanted to invoke the law of self preservation for himself.

> Much as I like Stanley Hack and wish him well,
> I wonder if he knows what's ahead for him? He, too,
> deserves a better fate. The Matthews uber alles
> setup ain't exactly Hack's proper level, either.[5]

Venerable Stan Hack guided the Cubs to a seventh-place berth. Wid promised that 1955 would be different and for half a season—including Bob Speake's great month of May—they held second place behind the Dodgers. Came the swoon—in July this time—and the season closed before they could drop lower than sixth. It took another year in the cellar before Jim Gallagher, Wid Matthews and Stan Hack were fired in favor of Charlie Grimm, John Holland and Bob Scheffing. Wid left shaking his head and muttering about seven years of bad luck.

John Holland cleaned house, dressed the 1957 Cubs in new uniforms and beat out Pittsburgh for seventh place by one game. A tie for fifth in 1958 and fifth by themselves in 1959, despite two straight MVP years from Ernie Banks, led to Charlie Grimm being named manager as successor to Bob Scheffing.

This time Charlie's magic didn't work and after 16 games, he was mercifully relieved by Lou Boudreau in a trade between the Cubs and WGN. When Boudreau, after a 64–90 record in 1960, asked for a two-year contract, all the elements were there for the infamous College of Coaches.

On January 12, 1961 it was announced that the Cubs would not have a manager for the 1961 season. Sportswriter Jim Enright noted that the Cubs had been doing without players for years and it was only fair that now they try it without a manager. Instead of a manager, the Cubs would be led by eight coaches including a "head coach" under a rotating plan. **As I wrote in *The Game Is Never Over:***

Even Cubs' General Manager John Holland admitted that when he had first heard the idea he thought Wrigley was nuts. But there was some logic in the system. In the first place, the system was not set up simply for the major league Cubs. The idea was to hire first-rate coaches for infielders, outfielders, and pitchers and to send them from top to bottom in the system to give uniform instructions. Every player in the organization received a manual explaining how the Cubs play baseball, how the Cub system works. "This is the day of specialists," Wrigley pointed out. "It makes sense to get the best man for each job. It works in football; I don't see why it can't work in baseball." He added, "We certainly cannot do much worse trying a new system than we have done for many years under the old."

Secondly, the system was devised to speed up the development of the young players in the farm system. The college of coaches would have personal knowledge of the strengths and weaknesses of each player and could consult with one another on their individual progress. Initially, there were to be eight coaches: Rip Collins, Vedie Himsl, Harry Craft, El Tappe, Gordie Holt, Charlie Grimm, Verlon Walker, and Bobby Adams. Speaking of the selection of these pioneers, John Holland had said, "We had to be careful. We couldn't hire a Durocher or Stanky, although they're good baseball men. We didn't want the type of guy who wants it done his way or else. We needed harmony, men who can be overruled and not take it personally. We needed men of varying capabilities and personalities. And that's what we got." The plan was that there would always be four coaches with the

Cubs and four circulating throughout the minors. The rotation of the head coaches would be maintained. Holland guaranteed that "no one man will run the Cubs this season, no matter how well he's doing. In fact, Mr. Wrigley said he'd love to see a head coach win nine straight and then step down. I'm sure that won't happen, at least not this year." Leo Durocher, then a coach with the Dodgers, said the plan really wasn't a bad idea. Thanks, Leo. But Bill Veeck, asked if he would follow suit and hire eight coaches to run the White Sox, said, "No, I'll go along with tradition. I guess I'm just an old stick-in-the-mud."

Everyone had his laugh, and soon it was time for spring training. The Cub players went on record as liking the new system. One said that he felt more relaxed and another that he worked harder than ever. The coaches certainly sang its praises. El Tappe thought it "the best thing that's happened to baseball since the spitball." And Gordie Holt reasoned that since there would always be four coaches with the Cubs at any given time "we'll have the advantage—we'll have four minds working and the other teams only one." Harry Craft reported, "I see no flaws. The plan has created harmony." Catcher Sammy Taylor summed it up, tongue-in-cheek, "My Lord, I can't even belch without one of the coaches hearing it."

In March, Mr. Wrigley added a further wrinkle. Since everyone from Ernie Banks to the newest kid on a class C team would be getting the same instruction from the revolving coaches, the word *minor* would be erased from the Cub vocabulary. "A player in the organization is a Cub no matter where he plays." A wag suggested that the Cubs should keep the word *minor* and banish the term *major* instead.

As spring training continued, everyone was anxious

to prove himself. Reports glowed with pitchers so ready and willing to start the season they almost had to be restrained. Billy Williams was slated to start in the outfield, Santo was ready for his first full season at third, young speedster Al Heist would be in center. Moe Drabowsky, who had pitched only fifty innings in 1960, was sent to Milwaukee for infielder Andre Rodgers. Just prior to the opening game, in a plane flight over Texas, Vedie Himsl was appointed head coach and given two weeks' notice at the same time. All four coaches would have a vote on the starting lineup, but once the game began, the head coach would be in charge. The Cubs lost the opener to the Reds, 7–2, and made it two in a row the next day, falling 5–2. Then, on April 14, with two outs in the ninth, catcher Sammy Taylor hit a two-run homer to beat the Braves, and the next day with the score knotted at 5–5, Al Heist grandslammed in the ninth for a victory. A week later, Don Zimmer homered with two out in the eleventh for a 6–4 win over the Phillies. Himsl finished his two weeks with a 5–6 record and headed for San Antonio; Harry Craft was the new head coach. After winning four of twelve games, Craft and Himsl traded places. By May 15 the Cubs were 10–17, in seventh place.

During the month of May, Mr. Wrigley issued a twenty-one-page, 5000-word defense of the no-manager plan. It began, "We have started out under an extreme handicap because of all the ridicule and criticism from the press at daring to try something different in baseball." (The press had dubbed the college the "enigmatic eight.") Wrigley went on to point out that in the last fourteen years, there had been 103 managers in the big leagues. Clearly managers and their coaches are expendable. But the constant changeover creates a loss of continuity. According to Wrigley, the Cubs' new system was designed to get

first-rate coaching and instructional ability in the organization from top to bottom, thus insuring continuity.
Obviously, the plan could only be judged from the perspective of several years. Would continuity be achieved?
Would it help develop stars more rapidly? Only time
would tell.[6]

Time told, all right! A 64–90 record landed Chicago
in seventh place. Cub infielder Don Zimmer, claimed by
the Mets in the expansion draft, left with a parting shot:

"Next year when I'm with the Mets I'll look over at
all my friends on the Chicago bench and feel sorry for
them. They don't have a chance to do their best." He said
that the coaches were competing with one another. "I've
seen one coach wagging Santo to play deeper at third
while another was motioning to him to come in further.
They are driving him crazy."[7]

**Years later, Billy Williams in an interview by Bob
Ibach, confirmed this:**

"If one coach liked a particular player he would
be in the lineup and the other guy was out," remembered Williams. "It all depended on who was the
head coach. In that respect the rotating coaching
system didn't work out. There was too much shuf-
fling going on . . . I just don't see how such a system
could ever work out in professional baseball."
When Williams first heard of the plan in spring
training, his reaction was one of shock and amusement. His teammates, Billy claimed, laughed too.
"Each guy (coach) was somewhat jealous of the
other one because everybody wanted to do good as

the head coach," said Williams. "I'm sure that some of them thought if they did a good job for a month they might get the job for another month. That's only human nature. It all added up to a lot of confusion for us.

"I remember this one game in particular when the head coach got ejected from the game. For the rest of the day the other coaches were passing around the hat making decisions.

"Santo, Banks and myself used to sit around and say 'this horsefeathers isn't going to work'. But everybody was tryin' to make it work because the old man (Wrigley) had proposed the idea."[8]

Wrigley stuck with the system for another season and the Cubs responded by finishing ninth in the 10-team league. Only the Mets were worse. For two and a half seasons Bob Kennedy was the sole "head Coach" and the Cubs hung around the lower third of the standings. But then Mr. Wrigley tried another desperate move: he hired Leo Durocher, the antithesis of the staid Cub image, and welcomed him into the family. Asked about Leo's penchant for loud and colorful language, Mr. Wrigley came up with the stunning rejoinder: "Well, Mr. Durocher is Mr. Durocher. What do you want, good taste or a good manager?"

-6-

WAIT 'TIL
NEXT YEAR (Or So)

Durocher endured a 10th-place humiliation in his first season with the Cubs. But destiny was driving the Cubs toward one of the most incredible seasons in their history. The cast had been assembled: Banks, Williams, Santo, Kessinger, Beckert, Hundley, Hands, Jenkins, Holtzman, Regan, Hickman—the Chicago boys of summer. After third place tuneups in 1967 and 1968, it was time for pennant fever. Wrigley Field rocked to full crowds for the first time in 20 years.

Eddie Gold and Art Ahrens said it perfectly:

> Then came euphoria. For most of the year, 1969 was the kind of season every Cub fan dreamed about. It was the year of Willie Smith's game-winning homer on opening day . . . Ron Santo clicking his heels after every home victory . . . Dick Selma leading the yellow-helmeted Bleacher Bums in cheers . . . Durocher saying "How 'bout another Slitz, fellas" . . . the "Hey Hey Holy Mackerel" song . . . the free Cub photos in the supermarkets . . . Ken Holtzman's no-hitter . . . a (then) club record 1,674,993 home attendance.[1]

Let us make a long and painful story short and painful. On July 1, the Cubs were 49–27, seven games ahead of the Mets. A week later, leading the Mets 3–1 in the ninth the Cubs blew the game when Don Young mis-played two fly balls inciting a Mets' rally. Both Durocher and Santo blasted Young and tension began to catch up with the Cubs. So did the Mets who took two of three from the Cubs in New York and the same in Chicago a few days later.

The Cubs clung to their lead into September, but on September 10, the hated Mets blazened on their score-board that they had taken over the top.

What had happened? **In *The Game Is Never Over*, I wrote:**

A great variety of theories have been advanced to explain the Cubs' swoon. A psychiatrist opined that the Cubs may have had an unconscious drive to lose the pennant. He said they were like school kids who do well for a good part of the year, only to take a good look at their grades, panic, and fail. Another theory was that the Cubs were so distracted by the outside interests generated by their success that they lost their concentration. They did have a team agent named Jack Childers who was in charge of building up a huge pot from endorsements, a pot the players split at the end of the season.

But most of the theories focused on Durocher himself. His constant feud with sportswriters cre-ated a tense atmosphere in the clubhouse. So did his willingness to publicly berate his players after a mistake. Many of the players disliked him for this, resenting the way he seemed to have absolutely no regard for people's feelings. For Leo, winning was everything. He didn't care whether he was liked or not. He criticized and ridiculed writers, coaches,

Lest we forget: Ron Santo and the Black Cat at Shea Stadium in 1969.

and players alike. It was even said that he had informants among the second stringers so that no clubhouse conversation was really safe from his hearing. Twice during the season he had taken off without even telling his coaches that he would miss a game or two. Such behavior seemed a measure of his respect for the players. When the pennant race got tight, the players had to tread too lightly around Leo. Little wonder if they treaded lightly on the field as well.[2]

Veteran writer Bob Logan saw it this way:

Ah, Durocher. Always in the eye of the hurricane. The Bleacher Bums went into hysterics at first glimpse of their leader, the number 2 on his back, emerging from the home clubhouse in the left field corner. Surrounded by a supporting cast of writers, coaches, and assorted hangers-on, the Great One would stride majestically to the dugout, pretending not to hear the Bums bawl adoringly:

Gimme that old-time Durocher,
Gimme that old-time Durocher,
Gimme that old-time Durocher!
It's good enough for me!

Despite all of Durocher's superstitions ("Everybody had to sit in the same place on the bench, and heaven help a batboy if he got two bats crossed," Selma recalled), his Cubs weren't good enough. While the Miracle Mets streaked, the snake-bitten Cubs were dissolving in a welter of name-calling and finger-pointing acrimony.

After it was all over and the Mets had thundered

Sadness Day. Mets' scoreboard on September 10, 1969.

past to take the Eastern Division title, knock off Atlanta in the first NL playoff, and stun the favored Baltimore Orioles in the World Series, the real Durocher emerged. The manager complained that the players had quit on him—not on the field, but by stepping out for a few late drinks in Montreal.

Chicago media people also served as a handy target. Leo had been feuding with the baseball writers over his habit of answering postgame questions with grunts while saving the inside story for radio and TV sycophants. On the tube and before a banquet audience, Durocher was at his best, charming the pants off the listeners, taking them into his confidence with gossipy anecdotes, and sending them home laughing at his fund of ribald humor.

Naturally, the fans loved him. Until the day he left Chicago after 6½ stormy seasons at the Cub's helm, Leo was their favorite, the man who deserved full credit for bringing excitement back to Wrigley Field. Virtually immune from criticism with the strong backing of owner Wrigley, Leo's ego finally betrayed him. He picked unnecessary feuds with two Windy City institutions: broadcaster Jack Brickhouse and Cub first baseman Ernie Banks. Mr. Cub wouldn't defend himself against the manager's sneering asides ("He's a rally-killer"), but Brickhouse would and did.

"There was a time when Leo was one of the greatest intuitive baseball men ever," Brickhouse said. "Nobody had to tell him his starter had thrown 90 pitches. He watched them like a hawk and he had that instinct for when a pitcher's ready to be pulled.

"In his earlier managing days, Leo had the heart of a gambler. The Leo who came to the Cubs was beginning to lose some of that. Before it was over, he had lost the rest."[3]

In his autobiography, *Thanks For Listening!*, Jack Brickhouse elaborated:

I objected to the way Leo handled Ernie Banks. He disliked Ernie from the go. It was just that Ernie was too big a name in Chicago to suit Durocher. Ernie Banks was and is the most popular athlete ever to put on a uniform in this city and I am positive Leo objected to Ernie's tremendous popularity with the fans.

He did his best, I felt, to break down Ernie's spirit, but no man can break a spirit like that.

I remember the game, at the tail end of Banks' career, that he let Ernie bat against a sidearming right-hander, then put in another right-handed hitter, Jim Hickman, as a pinch-hitter for Banks with a left-hander on the mound. Hickman told me later it was one of the toughest things he ever had to do.

In 1970, the Cubs closed out the season at New York and it appeared that this would be Banks' final game as a player. Leo withheld him from the lineup. It was a slap in the face. The fact that Ernie wound up making token appearances in 1971 is beside the point.

Well, I guess all that stuff is water over the dam now. To this day, I still don't send Leo a Christmas card. That makes us even. He doesn't send me one, either. No way.[4]

Over the winter, the Cubs' brain trust decided that all Cub regulars would take mineral baths at Buckhorn Spa for a week in preparation for spring training. But 1969 was not a spot that would wash away or a wound that would heal that easily.

The 1970 race was hindered by the loss of Randy Hundley for half of the season. The Cubs could not catch the Pirates and had to settle for second again. More frustration. Shortly before the end of the following season and with only a third place finish in sight, the tensions between the players and Durocher erupted during a clubhouse meeting. Leo insulted and demeaned the starters one by one and eventually Ron Santo had to be restrained from charging him. Leo quit, but relented when John Holland asked him to stay on. According to Fergie Jenkins, from then on "it was like an armed truce, like someone had pulled a blanket with 'death' written on it over the team." When the Cubs lost nine of their next 13 games, Mr. Wrigley took an ad in the Chicago papers telling the "Dump Durocher Clique" to give up; Leo was staying.

Well, he did until July 25 of the following season when Leo finally stepped down in favor of Whitey Lockman who led the Cubs from fourth to second by season's end.

By 1974 only Williams and Kessinger remained from the powerhouse Cubs of 1969. Once again Chicago slipped into the shadows of the league and became a whipping boy. Lockman turned the reins over to Jim Marshall but there was no avoiding a last-place showing. A year later Marshall's marshmallows managed to tie the Expos for fifth. In 1976 Bill Madlock won his second straight batting title, but there wasn't much else to cheer about. **Armand Schneider wrote in July of that year:**

NEW YORK—Laughter echoed from the Pittsburgh Pirates' dressing room the other night as a

(Illustration by John Trever)

boisterous argument took place following a 10–1 win over the Cubs.

"It took us one minute and 30 seconds to score," one of the players shouted.

"You're full of bleep," roared another. "It was a minute and 20 seconds."

Such was the indictment of the Cubs' pitching staff. It is bad and the reasons it is bad, with a disgraceful 4.91 earned run average going into the Met series that started here Friday night, are almost limitless according to experts who have watched them in action.

For obvious reasons, two of these baseball men will remain nameless. They are respected scouts for major league teams.

Scout A: "I would rate the pitching talent on this club 22d of the 24 teams in the majors. The thing I've noticed over the years is not so much the lack of 'stuff' but the lack of consistency. You can't have pitchers who have one good day, then three bad days."

Cubs' manager Jim Marshall: "We have a definite need for pitching. It would have to be rated in the lower echelon. I don't like to be negative, but the depth is not there. Consistency has been lacking."

Pitching coach Marv Grissom: "The earned run average is determined by the eight players behind the pitcher."

"Are there major league arms on this staff?" Grissom was asked.

Grissom paused and bit off a little smile. "They're here (in the majors), aren't they?" he answered.

Scout B—"It goes way back, starting with the trades of Fergie Jenkins and Ken Holtzman. They were good trades in themselves (for Bill Madlock and Rick Monday), but you have to make damn sure you have (pitchers) to replace them in quality. Then they traded (Burt) Hooton for a Geoff Zahn who is unable to pitch physically. They get a Dave LaRoche, then give him up for a Milt Wilcox (who is now in Evansville and out of the system). And they give up a Jim Todd for some odd reason and instead of a pitcher get John Summers. They get Mike Garman to get rid of an unhappy Don Kessinger, but could have done better if they weren't so eager to get rid of the unhappy player."

Scout A: "None of your (Cub) pitchers are capable of winning 20 to 22 games a season. The best of them, (Rick) Reuschel, (Bill) Bonham and (Ray) Burris are only going to be a few games over .500. I call it lack of command . . . an all-encompassing word. It's knowing where the pitch is going (control), poise, confidence."[5]

Time for a change. Back came Bob Kennedy, this time as vice-president in charge of baseball operations. And with Kennedy came the new manager, Herman Franks. Kennedy acquired Buckner and De Jesus for Monday but then sent Bill Madlock to the Giants for Murcer and Ontiveros. He got into the habit of defending his deals by gesturing that his hands were tied by Mr. Wrigley.

The fact is that the new Cubs of 1977 put on a surge the likes of which had not been seen at Wrigley Field for five years. By the end of June, they had a 47–24 record and a 7½ game lead on the rest of the league. Columnist George Will rhapsodized:

"HAVE YOU EVER KNOWN A YANKEE FAN WITH REAL CHARACTER?"
by George F. Will

At 7:17 A.M. (the moment is forever fixed in my memory) the drowsy stillness of the Will house was broken only by the voice of Ray Gandolf, the reporter of sports for the CBS morning news, giving baseball scores: " . . . the mighty Cubs beat . . ."

Mighty Chicago Cubs? I have waited decades to hear a sportscaster say something like that.

Unpleasant people say the Cubs are like Hilaire Belloc's water beetle:

> He flabbergasts the Human Race
> By gliding on the water's face
> With ease, celerity and grace;
> *But if he ever stopped to think*
> *Of how he did it, he would sink.*

Stuff and nonsense. The Cubs' sudden ascent to greatness is the work of Providence. In the fullness of time it has come to pass, as the prophets prophesied: the meek, who have eaten the bread of affliction, are inheriting the earth.

The romantic saga of the rampant Cubs is a nice counterpoint to unromantic baseball news, such as the trade of Tom Seaver from the New York Mets to the Cincinnati Reds. The Seaver trade, and the restless mobility of "free agent" superstars, strains fan loyalty. Baseball is a business but such unsentimental capitalism is bad business. Baseball capitalism that respects only market forces is profoundly destructive because it dissolves the glue of sentiment that binds fans to teams. Besides, as Jacques

Barzun says, baseball is Greek because it is based on "rivalries of city-states." Athens would not have traded Pericles for Sparta's whole infield.

Scholars concede but cannot explain the amazing chemistry of Cub fans' loyalty. But their unique steadfastness through thin and thin has something to do with the team's Franciscan simplicity.

The Cubs play on real grass, under real sunlight. Their scoreboard does not explode and they do not wear gaudy uniforms like those that have the Pittsburgh Pirates looking like the softball team from Ralph's Bar and Grill.

Iron has entered into the soul of this generation of Cub fans. World War II made the National League safe for the Cubs (they won in 1945, conscription having taken the able-bodied opposition), but since then, rooting for the Cubs has been the moral equivalent of war: hell. I became a Cub fan in Champaign, Illinois, in my seventh year, 1948, the year the Cubs management ran newspaper ads apologizing for the team. Thereafter, my youth was spent devising theories to take the sting out of summer.

One theory was that a .217 hitter was not a .217 hitter, he was a .295 hitter who really was, as broadcasters say, "overdue" for a hit. Never mind that most .217 hitters retired "overdue." Another theory was that each team would score only a certain number of runs each season, so when the Cubs lost twenty-two to nothing the winner squandered twenty-one of its allotted runs.

Baseball always was a sober experience for me. My friends played on Little League teams like the Piggly Wiggly Pirates and their colors were peppy red or green or blue. We on the Mittendorf Funeral Home Panthers wore black. Many children who had been trusted playmates revealed shocking flimsiness of character: they sank to rooting for the St. Louis Cardinals. I regarded these opportunities with lofty disdain, as De Gaulle regarded Vichyites. But now I know they were more to be pitied than censured, because rooting for a successful team is ruinous.

Have you ever known a Yankee fan with real character? Twenty years ago rooting for the Yankees was like rooting for IBM. It was for icky children who liked violin lessons and dreamed of being secretary of the treasury. What do Yankee fans know of the short and simple annals of the poor? Of lives of quiet desperation?

The most that can be said for most team loyalties is that they are poor preparation for here or the Hereafter. But rooting for the old, unregenerate Cubs was a complete moral education.

From 1946 through 1966 they finished seventh seven times and eighth six times. In 1962, the first year it was possible to finish ninth, the Cubs did, and the Mets had to extend themselves to a record 120 losses to wrest tenth from the Cubs. In 1966 the Cubs became the first nonexpansion team to finish tenth.

In those days, Cardinal fans reading *Who's Who in Baseball* found glowing descriptions of Stan Musial and Marty Marion. Cub fans read about their Lenny Merullo: "He is always on the verge of being ousted from his job because of his frequent erraticness—but he probably will be around this season." Bill Nicholson: "He has been in the clutches of a prolonged batting slump for three seasons." Paul Minner: "His wins were meager, but his stamina tremendous." Dutch McCall: He suffered from "disheartening support—and lack of endurance." Roy Smalley: "His errors at short are many, but he keeps trying." And Ralph Hamner: "The tall stringy hurler abounds in tough luck."

The Cub teams of this era taught their fans an invaluable lesson about the inevitable triumph of ineptitude over sincerity. From these Cubs we learned life's bitterest truth: the race *is* to the swift. Cub fans have seen a relief pitcher stride to the mound, promptly injure himself by falling off the mound and leave without having thrown a pitch. Today, a quarter of a century later, I am an embattled parent, convinced that babies are born plump as peaches because they are packed full of dubious ideas. It is never too soon for them to learn that the world is not their oyster, and *nothing* teaches that lesson quicker than loyalty to a train wreck like the 1948 Cubs.

Still, one summer of happiness can't do irreparable harm to me or the two rising Cub fans at the Will house. Yes, the paths of glory lead but to the grave, but so do all other paths. Yes, we bring nothing into the world and can take nothing out, but Ray Gandolf's sweet reference to "the mighty Cubs" is one thing no one can take away from us.

[*June 27, 1977*]

© *1978, Washington Post Writers Group. Reprinted with permission.*

But early in July the incredible Bruce Sutter was sidelined and Cub hopes went with him—all the way down to fourth. Armed with Dave Kingman, about whom the less said the better, the Cubs climbed to third in 1978 and they stayed in the race until September in 1979. But they then proceeded to lose 14 of 17 games in a swoon that mercifully halted at fifth. With but a week to go in the season, crusty Herman Franks abandoned ship and from his lifeboat shouted insults at Buckner, Vail, Sizemore, Foote and others. "Some of these guys are actually crazy," he said.

The Cubs would enter 1980 led by Preston Gomez and with the likes of Lenny Randle, Ken Henderson, Carlos Lezcano, Tim Blackwell and Dave Kingman as starters. Gomez was liberated on July 25 and left with the immortal words: "If I had known last winter what I know now, there is no way I would have taken this job." Joe Amalfitano had to witness the rest of the season, the third worst, at 64–98, by a Cub team since 1900.

The 1981 Cubs were reckoned by some to be the worst team in the history of baseball with the possible exception of the early Mets. Bob Kennedy's five-year plan was an abject flop and in May he was fired. Guess who came back to replace him? Herman Franks! That was the lowest moment in my life as a Cub fan. Apparently lots of people felt the same way. Fans started wearing T-shirts saying "Cub Fever—Catch it and Die." Signs were held up in the stands at Wrigley Field pleading with the owner, "Double your pleasure, double your fun. Sell the Cubs in '81."

And he did!

150

Every Tom, Dick and Harry knows you can't go wrong with "The World's Greatest Newspaper."

Here's to the North Side of Chicago's Greatest Team!

Credit: St. Louis Globe Democrat

Of course the Tribune bought the Cubs!

— 7 —

TRIBUNE AND TRIUMPH

On June 12, 1981, just hours after Herman Franks sold the Cubs' best pitcher, Rick Reuschel, to the Yankees, the Players Union called a strike and the season screeched to a halt. Cub fans were relieved. Four days later, they were shocked. William Wrigley announced that he had agreed to sell his 81 percent of Cub stock to the Tribune Company, thus ending a 66-year association between the Wrigley family and the Cubs. In true Wrigley fashion, William accepted the Tribune offer without trying to solicit higher bids because he felt that Tribune ownership would be best for the Cubs and for Chicago. Negotiations were conducted by Andy McKenna who had helped save the White Sox for Chicago a few years earlier.

The strike ended in August and the Cubs climbed ahead of the Pirates into fifth place for the second half. When league officials finally approved the sale of the Cubs, Andy McKenna, now chairman of the board, went looking for a new leader. He came back with Dallas Green. Jimmy Piersall welcomed Green to Chicago: "You have 14 guys who can't play Triple-A, the free-agent pickings are slim, and there's nothing in the minors. Good luck!"

It took Dallas only two years to make the wholesale changes needed to create a winner. But he did it. Against the odds, he did it! Lee Elia and Charlie Fox came and went before Jim Frey signed on as field manager for 1984.

In spring training it looked like more of the same. Fly balls were dropping and the Cubs were losing regularly. But there was one difference. Remember how Anson's Cubs, Chance's Cubs and Grimm's Cubs were known as fighters? On March 22, Fred Mitchell reported in the *Chicago Tribune*:

ROUND 2 AT CUBS' CAMP
This Time, Hall and Ruthven Exchange Haymakers
By Fred Mitchell

YUMA, Ariz.—When the Cubs aren't boxing grounders and routine fly balls, they're boxing each other.

Tuesday, the second fight this spring in the Cubs' camp erupted. The latest combatants were second-year light heavyweight center fielder Mel Hall and veteran junior middleweight pitcher Dick Ruthven. As baseball fights go, it was a dandy.

The two landed a couple of haymakers to the head in their fight behind second base during batting practice. Later, the San Diego Padres KO'd the Cubs 5–2 in an exhibition contest at lively Desert Sun Stadium.

Sportswriters judged the fight "even."

Last Friday, rookie welterweight pitchers Bill Johnson and Reggie Patterson—a couple of relative unknowns on the boxing horizon—were on the main event. With the Cubs, infighting is in.

If one word could describe the history of the Cubs . . .
(Photo credit: Stephen Green)

By the by, the Padres won Tuesday's game on former Cub Carmelo Martinez's three-run, two-out home run off Lee Smith in the ninth inning. That left the Cubs with a 3–11 preseason record, the worst ledger in the Cactus League.

But let's get back to main topic. Nearly a dozen teammates piled on to break up Tuesday's one-rounder, adding to the pregame entertainment for the handful of early-arriving fans. Yuma seldom has seen such excitement.

"Nobody's going to have a fight without me getting in the middle of it," said feisty rookie infielder Dan Rohn. Don King reportedly is considering arranging the next Cubs' bout in Las Vegas as a preliminary to the next Larry Holmes fight.

"An astrologer from San Francisco knew what he was talking about in January when he predicted the Cubs would experience fighting and turmoil in the clubhouse early in the season."

"But we're not even in the clubhouse yet," said Rohn.

The astrologer also predicted the Cubs would contend for the championship in the second half of the season.

Well, maybe one out of two ain't bad.

"Dick was picking up baseballs that were hit out there behind second base and putting them in the basket, and he told Mel to pick 'em up, too," said catcher Jody Davis, who was one of the first to try to separate the two pugilists. "I don't know what else was said."

"I'm fine," said Hall, who refused to comment further on the fight. Ruthven retreated to the team bus with his handlers after the game and was unavailable for comment.

Cubs manager Jim Frey ordered Hall to cool off on a bench in the right-field bullpen. Then he immediately called a team meeting out in center field following batting practice.

"The gist of what I said is that we're down here to win ballgames and nothing else," said the irate first-year Chicago boss. "I don't want selfish, individualistic attitudes on this team. Anyone who can't go along with the program can go play with somebody else."

Frey talked individually with Hall and Ruthven after the fight.

"I know what happened, but I'm not going to say," said Frey. "I just heard some remarks of what people said. Everyone on this ballclub has individual problems. Everybody's got problems. If we're going to fight anybody, we'll fight other teams in the National League. Anything else is cheap and amateurish and selfish. There's no place for it."

"Sometimes it helps to have some fight and spirit on the team, but something like this can't help us now," said Cubs captain Larry Bowa. "That astrologer guy really knew what he was talking about."

"This is not the first fight I've seen on the baseball field. It's not the end of the world," said Frey.

Asked if he would discipline the next players who became involved in a fight, Frey said: "I don't make hypothetical decisions. But I won't stand for that kind of behavior."

Even so, with the sudden acquisition of Gary Matthews and Bob Dernier in late March, the Cubs came out of Arizona as a bona fide contender.

As they played well through May and into June, even the Cubs began to believe in the Cubs. On June 13, their faith was deepened when Sutcliffe, Frazier and Hassey arrived from Cleveland. All of America began to root for the perennial underdogs from Chicago. Except, of course, New Yorkers. In June syndicated columnist David Broder wrote:

IT'S SO EASY
WHEN YOU GET THE KNACK
by David Broder

PHILADELPHIA—At last, it is over.

No, not the Democratic presidential race. We are not talking trivia in this space today. We are talking baseball. We are talking Chicago Cubs baseball, first-class, first-place baseball, my friend. After 39 years of frustration and broken hearts, the Cub fans of this world are experiencing the joyful fulfillment of our dreams.

We have a team. And we owe it all to Ronald Reagan.

This is no myth. I have seen the miracle with my own eyes, and I am here to tell you it is for real.

Last Friday night, I saw the Cubs take over first place in the National League Eastern Division by defeating the Phillies, 12–3. The date was June 1, 1984. You can look it up. The team that perfected the art of the June Swoon for four decades finally has broken the habit. The new Cubs have invented the June Swoop, to be followed by a Pie-in-the-Sky July, a Robust August and, of course, a September to Remember.

Thank you, Mr. President.

The Cubs are Reagan's team. They have been ever since he "re-created" their games from the Western Union ticker while broadcasting in Des Moines. He may not know the throw-weight of an MX missile or the target for M1 monetary growth, but he can still recite the lineup of those great Cub teams of the '30s. Not even his press secretary, Jim Brady, a true Cub devotee, can beat the president when it comes to Wrigley Field reminiscences.

The Cubs are Reagan's kind of team. They prefer not to work nights. They believe the three hours of labor in the afternoon are enough for any job. They know the old ways are best. God intended baseball to be played on grass and under the sun, so they play it that way. They appreciate beautiful surroundings. There is no more gracious ball park than ivy-covered Wrigley Field.

All this made the Cubs and Ronald Reagan a perfect match—except that the Cubs were losers. They did not Stand Tall. They were, to tell the truth, permanently stoop-shouldered from the weight of all the other teams that seemed permanently etched into the standings above them.

But simple application of Reagan's principles has brought the Cubs out of their 39-year slump and headed them toward greatness.

The first principle is: If you can't lick 'em, get 'em to join you. The conversion of the Cubs began in the first year of the Reagan administration, when Dallas Green was persuaded to leave the Phillies and become general manger of the Cubs. It was the greatest switch since Reagan left the Democratic ranks and became a Republican.

Green, like Reagan, did not forget his old pals. In a series of trades rivaling anything Reagan has pulled off at Tip O'Neill's expense, Green has acquired half his starting lineup from the Phillies. That has not made him popular in Philadelphia, I learned. But after furnishing talent to other teams for 39 years with a generosity rivaled only by the American banks' aid to Mexico, Brazil and Argentina, the Cubs have finally learned that it is more blessed to hornswoggle than to be swoggle-horned.

The second principle is the baseball version of supply-side economics: Take care of the big boys with the big bats, and they will take care of you. The Cubs opened in Philadelphia with a lineup that had more .300 hitters than .200 whiffers.

Ex-Phillies Bob Dernier and Ryne Sandberg scored the first two runs of the game, but by the bottom of the fourth inning, the Phillies had tied it. In the old days, that was a certain portent of defeat. But the new Cubs play with the spirit of Grenada and the ghost of George Gipp. In the fifth and sixth, Sandberg hit successive homers, the Cubs moved out to a 6–2 lead, and the Phillies fell apart—just as the Cubs used to do.

There were five errors by five separate Phillie players, and in the eighth the Cubs batted around. In the bottom of that inning, Rick Reuschel, who has come back from injuries almost as severe as those Reagan suffered in the assassination attempt, finally tired. He allowed three singles and a walk, and left with one run in and the bases loaded with just one out.

Manager Jim Frey brought in Tim Stoddard as a relief pitcher. Stoddard is also new to the Cubs. When he was in Baltimore, he was, to put it kindly, unpredictable. All he did on this occasion was to get Len Matuszek, the Phils' power-hitting first baseman, to bounce into a double play and then strike out the side in the ninth.

There was a decorous celebration among the Cub fans present, not wishing to presume too much on the good humor for which the Philadelphia fans (30,000 in number) are famous—particularly when their team has lost. Inside, our rapture was complete.

On Saturday, I am compelled to report, the Phils ended

the Cubs' reign in first place by beating them, 3–2. But on Sunday, the Cubs regained the lead with an 11–2 laugher.

It's so easy when you get the knack.

As the Reagan ads say, "Now that we've finally turned it around, why would we ever turn back?"

© 1984, *Washington Post Writers Group. Reprinted with permission.*

Two months later, with the Cubs still in front, George Will began to sound like a liberal optimist:

CHICAGO'S FAVORITE SONS
George F. Will

Real men don't eat quiche? Real Chicagoans won't even eat veal. Red meat rare, please. Big-shouldered, wheat-stacking Chicago fancies itself hairy-chested. But it has a baseball team, named for baby bears, that has been a byword for wimpishness. However, the Cubs are now, to coin a phrase, back and standing tall. Their fans—gosh, how many there suddenly are—are sitting atop the world on a pink cloud with rainbows draped over their shoulders. The rest of you had better brace yourselves for a spate of sociology. To understand the peculiar fervor of Cubs fans you must understand Chicago's temperament.

Chicago accommodates high culture (perhaps America's finest university, finest symphony, finest novelist and, for its size, finest art museum) but does not wallow in it. One Cubs broadcaster once said on the air to another, "I picked up the *Sun-Times* this morning and saw Sparky Anderson's [then manager of the Cincinnati Reds] picture on the front page. I wondered, what's Sparky done to get his picture on the front page? It turns out it

wasn't Sparky at all. It was a writer named Saul Bellow
who won the Nobel Prize."

Bellow, the novelist, is one of my pinups (my only
pinup who cannot hit behind the runner). He moved
back to Chicago from New York, in part because of Chicago's healthily relaxed attitude about the literati. Chicago writers are not expected to declaim about everything under the sun. Joseph Epstein, a man of letters
living in the Chicago area, notes that when Susan Son-
tag gave a speech in New York announcing her recent
discovery that communism is a bad thing, she caused a
stir. It is inconceivable that Bellow would utter such a
banality, or that anyone in Chicago would notice if he
did.

Low Point: Augie March, one of Bellow's characters,
says with nice concision that Chicago is "not mitigated."
Chicago takes life neat: no ice, no water. One mayor told
his machine, truthfully, "I'll do any damned thing you
boys want me to do"—a thought often thought but ne'er
so well expressed. When someone asked a judge to re-
quire Sally Rand to wear something beneath her two
ostrich-feather fans she (a mediocre dancer but a great
entrepreneur) had bought on credit, the judge snorted,
"Some people would like to put pants on horses." That
was an opaque but very Chicago-like contribution to jur-
isprudence, which in Chicago has some built-in elastic.
Chicagoans used to carry $10 bills folded with their driv-
er's licenses to settle matters when they were stopped
for speeding. That is why Mort Sahl called the Outer
Drive "the last outpost of collective bargaining."

Chicago, wrote Nelson Algren, "has grown great on
bone-deep grudges." The deepest are against New York,
and not just because of decaying New York's insuffer-
able snootiness about thriving Chicago. There also is
the atrocity of Sept. 8, 1969, the low point of a low dec-

ade. I don't want to beat a dead horse to death but Tommie Agee was out at the plate that night.

The Cubs were in New York playing the Mets, a parvenu outfit that did not exist until 1962, when it lost a record 120 games. What was the first team to finish below the Mets? The 1966 Cubs. The Cubs still have not won a pennant since 1945, when all but the lame were fighting the Axis. But in 1969 the Cubs led the pack until a September swoon, the crucial moment of which was the first game of the two-game series the Mets swept. The Mets won it 3–2 when Agee scored from second on a single by a dinky .218 hitter. At least the umpire said he scored. I say the umpire's scandalous decision was the beginning of Watergate. The image of Agee scoring— a summation of all the insults visited on Chicago by New York—is burned on every Cubs fan's mental retina. The wound will not heal until there is mighty vengeance from the Midwest, perhaps this year.

Baseball is heaven's gift to struggling mortals, but has meant more thorns than roses for Chicago. The other team, the White Sox, has won only four pennants in 83 seasons. The 1919 "Black Sox" took a dive in the World Series. The 1906 "hitless wonders" had an anemic batting average of .228 but still managed to win the series, beating, who else?—the Cubs. It has been said that the test of a vocation is love of the drudgery it involves. Being a Cubs fan is a vocation because the memory of man runneth not to a time when rooting for the Cubs was not mostly drudgery.

Tribute: Today's Cubs are a tribute not to husbandry but to entrepreneurship. Few players were grown down on the Cubs' farm teams. Most were traded for by Dallas Green, an executive with the breezy eloquence of the Wife of Bath and the administrative flair of Lady Macbeth. Such wheeling and dealing strikes some purists as the summit of crassness, but this is a Republican era, so sharp practices are without moral taint.

A theory, contentedly expounded by the comfortable, is that suffering makes us spiritual. (John Wesley wrote to his sister Patty: "I believe the death of your children is a great instance of the goodness of God toward you. You have often mentioned to me how much of your time they took up! Now that time is restored to you . . . you have nothing to do but serve our Lord.") To those who say that passing through a fiery furnace is good for one's soul—that we learn in suffering what we teach in song—I say: one can have too much soul.

Real Cubs fans are 99.44 percent scar tissue. A fast start by the Cubs causes them no palpitations. Such feints are traditionally followed by faints. But now it is August and, wonder of wonders, the team is still in the thick of things. Dull despair has yielded to flaming hope, which is building like steam in a pressure cooker. Also, true Cubs fans are as mean as most winners unaccustomed to winning and are busy repelling late-boarders from their gravy train.

Remember, this year baseball is politics carried on by other means. And in America, politics is most bitter when what is at issue is status. The Cubs are William Jennings Bryan, a prairie uprising against highfalutin Eastern plutocrats wearing spats, the Mets and Phillies. "Arise ye prisoners of starvation!"—that is the Cubs' anthem.

Chicago, wrote Algren, is "an October sort of city even in spring." The numbed nerves of Cubs fans are sensing the possibility that this year it could be spring—resurrection, regeneration—in October.

[August 13, 1984]

Finally, it happened. On September 24, 1984 Rick Sutcliffe pitched a two-hit, 4–1 win over the Pirates and the long draught was over. At last the Cubs had a championship. *South Bend Tribune* sports editor and Cub fan Bill Moor said it as well as it could be said:

CALL THEM
THE FLUBS NO LONGER
by Bill Moor

Until last night, I hadn't sipped champagne since my wedding day. On a few occasions, I have told my wife that was the happiest day of my life.

I better leave it at that, but last night was a time to celebrate and cherish. The wait finally was over. The Cubs were champions.

Let me say that again, the Cubs were champions. The Chicago Cubs, those lovable and longtime losers who are responsible for 25 years of scar tissue on my heart, are champions. God does love them.

I sat there in front of the television and got goosebumps while I watched the Cubs—my Cubs flood the field and winning pitcher Rick Sutcliffe. I was with good company—a few old friends and Ernie Banks, a 1959 baseball card of Mr. Cub himself propped up beside me.

And yes, my three kids were dragged out of bed to witness this historical event. You never know. If history holds its course, it may be a long time before they see a Cub clinching again.

My five-year-old, awakened out of a sound slumber, must have thought he was seeing the end of the world as he stared at a bunch of guys jumping all over each other both on the television and in the living room.

Finally. September 24, 1984. (Photo credit: Sandy Bertog)

The magic number was finally down to zero after a countdown that lasted 39 years. It was a beautiful day for a ball game. Hey, hey and holy cow and let's play two tomorrow. The Cubs will not be in hibernation this October.

Flush the flubs title forever. Speak of September Swoons no more. Finally mention 1969 without hyperventilating.

To tell you the truth, I thought about 1969 a lot last night. When the Cubs popped the corks on the champagne, I figured that old Ern, Ron Santo, Billy Williams, Randy Hundley and the rest of those '69 Cubs were smiling somewhere. In my heart, they were a part of the celebration.

I like to think that some of the breaks that the 1969 team didn't get were inherited by this championship team—saved up all those years someplace where fairness isn't a fairytale.

It hasn't completely set in yet but last night was a monumental moment for Cub fans. A faithful follower for only a quarter of a century, I am a veritable rookie compared to some of the long-suffering Cub fans. Last night was their time to roar—and soar.

The last time I cried in public was when my dad had driven my brother and me to Wrigley Field for a late-season Cub-Cardinal doubleheader. The Cards were going for the 1964 pennant and the game was sold out before we got there. I sobbed right out there on the corner of Clark and Addison. I was a mess.

My dad, a little embarrassed by it all, nevertheless paid scalpers' prices for tickets so we could see the Cubs sweep the Cards. But the next evening, we had a little father-to-son chat about acting like a man.

I don't think I have cried in public since but maybe
it was just as well that it was raining cats and dogs
when I finally got home last night. Teardrops and
raindrops feel the same.

My wife, no Cub fan, wasn't in a celebrating mood
and had locked me out. "But this was the second
best day of my life," I told her when she finally came
to the door.

"The second best day of your life ended 2½ hours
ago," she said.

Maybe the third best day of my life had begun.[1]

The rest is, as they say, history. Joy unbounded in Chicago as the Cubs waltzed to two easy wins over the Padres in the playoffs. Then, riled by a column by Mike
Royko which heaped barbs on San Diego and its residents, Padres fans plus just plain angry San Diegoans
turned the tide. Instead of meeting ennui in San Diego, the
Cubs ran into an army of hostile fanatics. They shouted,
conducted repeated waves around Jack Murphy Stadium
and inspired the Padres to three straight wins and the
pennant. Next time, Royko, keep your thoughts to yourself.

It was a shock. It hurt. But fans like Bill Moor kept
it in perspective:

HEY, MOM, I DIDN'T EVEN CRY
by Bill Moor

Dear Mom,

I was a big boy. If watery eyes don't count, I didn't
even cry.

But I've got to tell you, Mom, that when I was out
there in the middle of all those San Diego Padre

fans, I felt about as lost as the time I got separated from you and Dad in the St. Louis zoo's monkey house. The monkeys were better company, too.

I know you watched Sunday's Cub loss even though I figure you like baseball about as much as balled socks in the laundry chute. But you've remained a faithful follower of the ball scores even if you had to doze through the weather to make it to the sports report.

You're a good and caring mother and you know that the Cub score is like a long-distance linkup to my heart—a heart with 26 years of scar tissue courtesy of the Cubs.

Mom, that heart was broken on Sunday. You knew that, though. Only you really know how important the Cubs have been to me over the years. And because of that, they became important to you, too.

You seemed to have the Cubs figured out better than I did, too. Remember how after every World Series, I would ask you if I could stay home from school if the Cubs got into the Series the next year? You always gave me one of those all-knowing smiles and said, "If the Cubs are in the World Series, you can have the flu."

I felt sick on Sunday, Mom, but it wasn't the flu. And I don't have to tell you that my fall attendance record during my school days was that of an Iron Man's.

Gosh, I really thought this was going to be the year. But even when they won the first two games of the National League playoffs, I bet you had your doubts—relying on history rather than headlines. Deep down, maybe I had some of those same doubts, too.

You'll tell me to look at the good side, though. You always have. At times, you've hinted to me why you've put up with the Cubs all these years. They've been good for me even when they haven't been good.

Mom, you once told me that Ernie Banks probably did more than you and Dad combined in helping me grow up pretty much prejudice-free.

You also quickly realized that 100-loss seasons could teach a youngster like me about not dwelling on setbacks too long. The Cubs were almost like the Cub Scouts—they taught me patience, persistence and true-blue loyalty. I guess they made me a dreamer and hopeless optimist, too.

And you knew long before I did that the Chicago Cubs are probably the main reason I'm a sports writer today. Poring over the boxscores and reading the accounts of the Cub games were what first drew me to the sports pages and kept my intrigue.

I know what you're going to say, Mom. You're right, you're right. I can be upset with the loss, but I shouldn't be with the Cubs.

And when I think about it, this has been a great year of baseball and the Cubs did win a title over a long season of outstanding play. You remember 1969, Mom? That's the year that I . . . no, I won't remind you of that. Well, this year can't be compared to that year. This year gave us a championship. This year was the best yet.

The Cubs took a big step this year. It would have been nice if it was a little bigger but maybe it will be next year. There's always next year, you know. Yeah, you know.

I'm starting to feel better already just writing this to you, Mom. In fact, I wasn't going to tell you this but I wore my Cub hat through the San Diego airport the morning after the Padres beat the Cubs for the pennant. A lot of Padre fans started to give me a hard time.

I stopped them in their tracks, though. "You're right," was my pat answer to all of them. "Your team was the best team. You should be very proud. My congratulations. I tip my hat to you."

After that, most of them stammered and stuttered and finally admitted the Cubs were pretty good, too. One even rushed up to me and apologized profusely for being such a bleep.

If I have learned one thing over the years, Mom, it's to be a good loser. And a good loser can many times make a poor winner feel two inches tall. I got revenge by speaking softly and smiling.

Hey, Mom, you even have me smiling now. I'm even ready to hear Ernie Banks' new chant for 1985. Start up the magic number.

The Cubs and I go back a long ways, Mom, but not as long as you and I do. Thanks for straightening me out. You might not believe this but I even love you more than the Cubs.

Your No. 1 son,
Bill

P.S.—Root for a Tiger sweep.[2]

New York Times columnist and now CBS New Correspondent, William E. Geist, writing in *Esquire*, captured the moment:

CUBS FEVER!
It's Terminal
by William E. Geist

My beloved grandfather told me in 1955 that while the Chicago Cubs had not won a pennant in ten years, I should stick with them. "The Cubs," he proclaimed, "will soon be back on top." He was lucky; he died that year. Some twenty-nine seasons later, while shaving, I recalled those words of my forefather and—perhaps because I finally felt old enough—responded: "My ass."

This was to have been a historic evening, a night to redefine celebration, to throw off the mantle of frustration, to baffle the neighbors by rollicking in quiet suburban Maryland, to drink, to shout, and perchance to get sick in the shrubs.

This was to be the night the Cubs clinched the National League pennant for the first time since 1945, when it seemed most other major leaguers were off fighting World War II. This may explain why Cubs fans tend to regard the prospect of World War III with a certain ambivalence.

Several dozen ebullient fans, carrying bottles of champagne and dressed in full Cubs regalia, crammed into the Kensington, Maryland, home of Bruce Ladd, lobbyist for a Chicago firm and Cubs fan extraordinaire. He has lived eight hundred miles from Chicago for twenty years by force of circumstance, but he manages to keep the faith, making regular pilgrimages to Wrigley Field, home of the Cubs.

He has raised his son to be a Cubs fan. It seems cruel. Fifteen-year-old Bruce Ladd III sat on the couch in a Cubs shirt and cap, just a short drive from the Baltimore Orioles, consistent winners and the logical local team for the boy to follow. "I have Cubs stickers on my locker at school," said the boy. "The other kids think I'm weird."

Fans at the party talked excitedly of their plans to attend the World Series that would be played the next weekend in Chicago, once the Cubs polished off the San Diego Padres in the play-offs. For a Cubs fan, a World Series can be a once-in-a-lifetime opportunity. There had been a sense of urgency just to see the Cubs winning during the regular season. Randy Lightle said that he and his bride drove, on their honeymoon, fourteen hours straight through from Washington to Chicago for standing-room-only tickets. "My wife wanted to go to Paris and London," he said, "but I told her that Paris and London would always be there."

Steve Garvey doubled in the third inning as the Padres took a 2–0 lead. The happy revelers in the Ladd home stopped talking. They moved to the edges of their chairs, pulled their Cubs caps down, and began watching in earnest. No National League team had ever won the first two play-off games, as the Cubs had, and then gone on to lose the five-game series. Yet theirs was a team of destiny.

Emil Verban, a former Cubs infielder from the 1940s, who set a record by hitting just one home run in his 2,911 at bats, gazed down upon the fans in Ladd's living room from an enlarged photograph over the mantel, a ghost of seasons past. This was a gathering of the Emil Verban Memorial Society, a group of Cubs fans mostly from the Washington, D.C., area that includes the likes of columnists George Will and David Broder, U.S. Supreme Court justices Blackmun and Stevens, at least a dozen U.S. senators and congressmen, and—right there on the society roster—number 144: "Ronald Reagan, President of the United States; The White House,

Washington, D.C. 20500." Reagan is a member because he broadcasted Cubs games on WHO radio in Des Moines, recreating the play-by-play from wire-service reports as if he were at the games. Sometimes the wires stopped and Reagan had no information, but he went right on with the lively broadcast as if he knew what he was talking about.

The Society holds a biannual meeting and bestows such honors as the Harry Chiti Look-alike Award, in honor of the corpulent former Cubs catcher, and the Brock-for-Broglio Judgment Award, commemorating a typical Cubs' trade of yesteryear that sent a young future all-star to another team in exchange for a gent in the dusk of his career.

More ghosts drifted up from the basement, where Ladd keeps the Society's archives, including such things as tickets to the 1969 Cubs play-off series, which failed to materialize when the Cubs folded in legendary fashion, and copies of the record "A Dying Cub Fan's Last Request," by Steve Goodman, the folk singer and Verban Society member, who had died at thirty-six, just days before the Cubs clinched their 1984 division title.

The Cubs went ahead 3–2 in the fourth inning and the capacity crowd in Ladd's house erupted like the bleacher section at Wrigley Field. There was even cheering from the bathrooms. TV sets were positioned in every room in the Ladd home because the fans wanted to savor every moment of the historic game and because this was a beer party.

Rabid followers of your Chairman Maos and Michael Jacksons come and go, but Cubs fans remain devoutly loyal, year after losing year, as the Cubs defy—and, indeed, have begun to undermine—all laws of mathematical probability.

How? "It makes all kinds of sense," said John Wimberly, a Presbyterian minister and Cubs fan at the party, "for someone who has spent his entire life following a man who was nailed to a cross to be a Chicago Cubs fan. The theology of all this is the nobility of suffering."

Cubs players who've been imported from other cities marvel at the local support, which was there even in 1983, when the Cubs finished fifth in their division. "In Los Angeles," third-baseman Ron Cey has said, "they expect you to win. In Chicago, they hope." The Chicago mind-set would seem the very opposite of New York's, where people who seem to have everything are always screwing themselves out of happiness by wanting more.

"Losing is not so bad," Ladd contended, "when you're accustomed to nothing else. It's the ups and downs in life that are bad."

Fans say that following the Cubs has taught them a philosophy of life: that we fail more often than we succeed, and still "tomorrow comes," as Jim Langford put it.

In Chicago it can seem as though it is not whether you win or lose, nor how you play the game. It is the appreciation of the game of baseball itself that is important, and of warm days, after long Chicago winters, out at the old ball park. "Cub fans," said Bill Hickman, "are more interested in the game than in jumping up and down yelling 'We're Number One!' People who do that aren't real baseball fans." Lest we forget: the Chicago White Sox last appeared in a World Series in 1959 and their previous appearance was in 1919. Chicago has not won a major sports title of any kind since 1963. After the Cubs and the Bears football team both came somewhat close during their last seasons, Mayor Washington went ahead and proclaimed Chicago "a city of champions."

"The Chicago Cubs, like life itself, are a losing cause,"

Mike Royko, columnist and number forty-nine on the Verban Society roster, told me. "That's why we have cemeteries. And Wrigley Field."

It is a common misconception, however, that Cubs fans somehow actually *enjoy* losing, that being a Cubs fan is some sort of self-deprecatory chic. "Screw *that!*" one Cubs fan commented rhetorically. Some fans compare watching the Cubs to classic tragicomedy. "We laugh," said one, "but it hurts." Many said they would be perfectly happy to become really obnoxious winners, like the old Yankee or Notre Dame football fans, swaggering into bars in other cities with their Cubs jackets on, bragging too loudly, and slopping drinks on other people's shoes.

Whether the fans could really do that after all these years—the Cubs were world champs last in 1908, when Orval Overall hurled them to victory—is another matter.

There were enough adjustment problems just to doing a little winning last season. "We became neurotic," said one fan, "worrying about getting tickets and about wining the important games. I'd never been to an important game."

Old-fan-syndrome developed. "I couldn't help it," said one Wrigley Field veteran at the party. "I'd see these Johnny-come-latelies jumping up and down, waving their pennants, and I'd think that I had suffered forty years for this, and that they didn't deserve it. They were probably backing the White Sox when they were winning last year."

"Long-suffering fans" at bars across the street from the ball park were interviewed so frequently that they complained it was cutting into their drinking time. Some sufferers were interviewed so often that they took to saying "cut" to TV crews. One group of fans that watch the games from the rooftops of buildings across the street refused to grant any more interviews, claiming that their comments had been "misrepresented in the press." Two residents of a building across the street from the ball park who had always watched games from the roof sued their landlord when he tried to rent their space out as a sort of corporate box.

And there was an adjustment to seeing all those ex-Phillies the Cubs had purchased running around out there in the field in Cubs uniforms like so many mercenaries hired to win a pennant. But that's the way it's done these days. The new owner of the team, the Tribune Company, has more than doubled the team's payroll, which under the niggardly ownership of the Wrigley family was running at about one hundred packs of Doublemint per annum. But in the end, these ex-Phillies and other imports would prove, in dramatic fashion, that they really had become Cubs through and through.

Steve Garvey singled in a run in the fifth inning to tie the score at 3–3. He singled in another run in the seventh, when the Padres took a 5–3 lead, and more ghosts stirred in the room. In the gathering silence before each pitch, one could almost hear the haunting Cubs roll call: Verle . . . Tiefenthaler; Cuno. . . .Barragan; Nineteen . . . Sixty-nine; Billy . . . Grabarkewitz . . . Johnny Boccabella; Oscar . . . Zamora. "When the pitch is so fat that the ball hits the bat, that's Zamora."

If some view following the Cubs as some crazed kamikaze-Jonestown type of clinical fandom, there are many others who see it as good old-fashioned commitment. Cubs fans disdainfully throw back homerun balls hit by opposing teams. Think of it! This would never happen in another city, certainly not in New York, where Madison Square Garden crowds gave Michael Jordan, the Chicago Bulls rookie sensation, standing ovations last winter as he was destroying their own Knicks.

There is a uniquely powerful bond between Cubs fans and their team, perhaps because the fans are closer in proximity to the players in the National League's smallest park—and perhaps because they are closer in ability. It has been said many times in many places that "a team is only as good as its fans," but at Wrigley Field some sort of annual play-off would seem appropriate.

Most Cubs fans got that way in childhood (as social service agencies stood idly by). They talked at the party about going to the park with their fathers, about playing hooky from school to attend the games, and recalled folding up seats and picking up popcorn boxes for free passes to the next day's game.

Ladd said that following the Cubs is a "nostalgia trip." There could be no better vehicle into the past.

The Cubs (then the White Stockings) won their first pennant back in 1876. Sitting in Wrigley Field today is like riding some great ghost ship with flags flying in the Chicago winds. The park itself has not changed since fans attended games there a generation or two ago—still with the brick, ivy-covered outfield wall, still with the manual scoreboard and the natural grass field. Fans don't do The Wave cheer at Wrigley Field.

"The Friendly Confines," as Wrigley Field is called, sit smack in the middle of a city neighborhood, as all ball parks once did, and home-run balls still crash through the windows of homes across the street.

Cubs games are played, as once all baseball was, "in God's own sunshine," as Ernie Banks said; "as the Good Lord intended," adds Cubs broadcaster Harry Caray. There is no parking, other than the very few V.I.P. spots, the streets and alleys, and just up the street at the Good

Shepherd Sisters convent, where—Sweet Jesus!—did the sisters ever make a killing last year.

"When you're a Cubs fan," said Langford, "you *can* go home again."

Champ Summers of the Padres swung at a hideously high fastball, and Ladd yelled, "Ex-Cub factor! Summers is an ex-Cub. No team in modern history has won the World Series with more than two ex-Cubs on the team roster." He points out, hopefully, that the Padres pitcher, Craig Lefferts, is also an ex-Cub.

Harry Caray points out at the slightest provocation that "you can't beat fun at the old ball park," and he means it. The old-fashioned broadcaster sometimes does the play-by-play from aisle 153 of the bleachers. He excitedly yells "Cubs win! Cubs win!" and he gets mad when they don't. He's just like the other fans, except that he probably drinks more beer during the game than they do.

Bill Veeck, patriarch of baseball, regularly sits out with his shirt off and his peg leg in the aisle. Veeck was a vendor at the park in 1924, when his father was president of the club, and in 1937 he planted the vines along the wall.

When Harry gurgles "Take Me Out to the Ball Game," during the seventh-inning stretch, and he gets to the part about "I don't care if I never get back," many of those fans sitting Zen-like in the sun with cold beers—a goodly number of them playing hooky from the office during the afternoon games—honestly don't care if they ever do.

"I lived in Houston for a while," pastor Wimberly told me at the party, "and the Astrodome is absolutely disgusting." If Houston is an Astro-Turf city, Chicago is all-natural.

"Chicago," said Royko, "is an old-fashioned, traditional American city, with subways and buses and neighborhoods with bungalows. The Cubs and Wrigley Field represent something to hang on to."

While watching the game the expatriates reminisced about their former Chicago neighborhoods, and talked fondly of Mayor Daley, vote fraud, the Blizzard of '79, Rush Street, the St. Patrick's Day Parade, and the uproar created when a large Picasso sculpture, which thousands of Chicagoans thought should have instead been a statue of Ernie Banks, was erected in The Loop.

"It's a comfortable city," said Ken Feltman, "that fits like an old shoe." Those who had lived elsewhere said they preferred Chicago to New York, which they found to be too dirty and too big; to Washington, where they said politics was all anyone could talk about; and certainly to Sun Belt cities, which they tend to view as suburban-style franchise operations. They particularly disliked San Diego, in part because it is the ground Steve Garvey walks on.

There is a growing antipathy between America's great old cities and those of the Sun Belt, and this play-off series pitted one against the other. The *San Diego Tribune* wrote in an editorial that Chicago is "a has-been slum of sausage-eaters on the toxic waste Riviera of America." Chicagoans didn't bother responding; it would be rather like beating a retarded child, wouldn't it?

In the eighth inning, the Cubs came back to tie the game. "I told you!" shrieked one of the newer fans. "These are the new Cubs!" The Space-age Cubs—beamed via satellite in 1984 on Superstation WGN throughout the free world! Places like the Key Largo Bar in Costa Rica became hangouts for Cubs fans.

Fans at the party discussed all the excuses over the

years for losing—from astrological to climatological— and the team's often bizarre attempts at solving its problems.

The fans said that one of the main problems was Philip K. Wrigley, who owned the Cubs from 1932 to 1977, a man they characterized as a nice guy perfectly capable of understanding a stick of gum.

The managers were always blamed, and in the early '60s the Cubs manager was replaced with the bizarre College of Coaches, whereby a different coach took over the team every couple of weeks. This approach helped the Cubs extend their string of second-division finishes to a record twenty seasons between 1947 and 1966. The torch was then passed to Leo Durocher, who pronounced, "This is not an eighth-place ball club." In his first year the Cubs finished tenth.

The debilitating heat—the Cubs having to play all their home games in the daytime—was a favorite excuse. But when lights were seriously proposed for the park, public outcry was so great that the state legislature passed a law effectively outlawing lights.

The Goat Theory came to the fore in recent years. William Sianis, once proprietor of the Billy Goat Tavern, which inspired John Belushi's "chizborger, chizborger" routine, is said to have put a hex on the Cubs in 1945 when his pet goat was not allowed into the park. His nephew ceremonially brought the restaurant's pet goat to Wrigley Field last year.

The Thermonuclear Fallout Theory seems to make the most sense, the first bombs having been dropped as the Cubs were clinching their last pennant.

In the ninth inning Steve Garvey stepped to the plate with the score tied and hit a dramatic home run to win the game for the Padres. At this point, something needs to be said about Steve Garvey: Cyndy Garvey left Steve for Marvin Hamlisch. One can imagine Steve's teammates stopping by his locker, patting him softly on the shoulder, and offering their condolences: "*Geez*, Steve, it must be rough. I mean *Marvin Hamlisch*—" and then walking away, shaking their bowed heads.

The ghost of P. K. Wrigley squatted over the punch bowl. The party was over. But Cub fans agreed there was still no way their team could lose the play-offs, not with Rick Sutcliffe, the best pitcher in the National League, with fifteen straight wins, taking the mound for the Cubs the next day in the final game.

"I know, I know," Ladd said, as he bid farewell to them at the front door. "But you start to see a kind of a poetry to the way this is going, you know?"

I purposely did not turn on the car radio for the first few innings of the final game. When I finally tuned in, the Cubs were winning 3–0, but within seconds, Sutcliffe faltered as he had not done all season. The electronic image of Leon Durham, Spaceage Cub, was beamed 22,300 miles above the equator to a satellite in geosynchronous orbit and bounced down to tens of millions of viewers who watched the ball skitter through his legs on a critical play. It was my fault. I was the one who just had to go and turn on the radio.

The Cubs lost 6–3, against all odds, writing another legendary chapter in team history. The mathematical inevitability had proved just another monumental challenge to the Cubs. Poetry.

As I drove back to New York on the New Jersey Turnpike, it occurred to me how grossly inaccurate was the *San Diego Tribune*'s depiction of the Chicago area as the toxic waste Riviera of America. It also occurred to me that the Cubs are fundamental in nature; that, yes, you can tinker with them, changing owners, managers, and coaches and buying stars from other teams, but the team is basically as unalterable as hydrogen, zinc, manganese, or any of the other stuff on the periodic table of elements.

The drive home was punctuated with a few deliberate swerves toward bridge abutments, but I managed a faint smile when it occurred to me just how awful the World Series would be without the Cubs. As readers may recall, it sucked.

Following the discontent of Chicago's winter, spring is a time of rejuvenation and new hope. Sprightly crocuses push their way through the tundra, and opening day at Wrigley Field approaches. Cubs fans look out at the little birds on their lawns after life-giving spring rains, and they imagine the birds thinking to themselves: "Why are we the ones God keeps choosing, year after year, to eat these slimy, goddamned worms?"[3]

After off years, riddled with memories of the playoffs and with physical injuries too, the Cubs were again open to less than flattering observations. Witness the following by Bob Verdi:

Bob Verdi
In the wake of the news
WINTER BASEBALL
IS CHICAGO'S BEST

Winter baseball has begun, and not a moment too soon for Chicago fans, who prefer it over the alternative because it is free of charge and statistics. As an example, when a pitching coach is fired on his hospital bed, this might be bad form, but it merely affects morale, not the standings.

Billy Connors was, however, only the second Cub chattel cashiered in 1986 while found in a compromising position. Marla Collins beat him to it, and she was wearing even less than a bandage at the time. Of course, if Dallas Green wanted to rid himself of every employee who drew a salary while lying down, he'd have few players left. Or, even fewer than he's got.

Be that as it may, Herm Starrette is the new arm doctor for the Cubs. He should be perfect for the job, having served in the National Guard. It doesn't take an earthquake or flood to precipitate disaster at Wrigley Field, of course, only a slight breeze blowing out in the top of the first inning. Whatever, it never hurts to have a man overqualified for his position. At least Starrette, a one-game winner in the major leagues, hasn't been presented to us as "sticking out like a sore thumb." What he might have around August, after all those trips to the mound, is sore feet. We wish him godspeed and a strong stomach.

The Cubs also have refurbished their mess of '86 by acquiring Jimmy Piersall. At age 56, Piersall still is the best defensive outfielder on the payroll. However, his role has been defined as community relations. The Cubs are much beloved in communities throughout the National League; his mission is to make them more beloved here. Specifically, Piersall will deal with what the Cubs are doing about mental illness and drug use. That is, what the Cubs are doing about combating those problems, not creating them.

It is said that one of Piersall's first priorities these days—nothing to do with his new title—is launching legal action against Jerry Reinsdorf and Eddie Einhorn for calling him "scum" after the White Sox won half a pennant in 1983. Harry Caray, once Piersall's broadcast partner on the South Side, was also included in that blast by the Sox co-owners, who surely have enough public relations problems of their own. "We can't afford any more mistakes," said Reinsdorf, alluding to his team's announcement that the Sox's new general manager will be Larry Himes, who served the California Angels well. The Sox are operating on a sound theory here: If you can't beat them, rob them.

Whether Chicago's twin Titanics will extend that philosophy to the free-agent market is another matter. Green already has pledged that he'll not buy anybody else's athletes, having lost enough sleep and games with his own. The White Sox haven't really come forth with a statement of policy, other than to promise that credibility shall return to the franchise after a short sabbatical. The White Sox will bear watching in upcoming months, and again, that will be easier than during the summer. You don't need to find a bar with SportsVision.

Certainly, all of baseball will scrutinize winter activity. Club bosses got by last year claiming a lack of quality and quantity in the free-agent pool. But this year, the talent is estimable: Jack Morris and Lance Parrish of the Detroit Tigers, Tim Raines and Andre Dawson of the Montreal Expos, Jack Clark of the St. Louis Cardinals, Bob Horner of the Atlanta Braves, to name just a few. If no opposing team nibbles, if these stars are courted only by their existing employers, the players' association will scream anew about collusion and conspiracy. The

owners must be careful, because already a griev-
ance has been lodged about the curiously passive
winter of '85.

Not all improvements must result from outright
outbidding, however. A little homework helps. For
instance, if the Expos opt to re-sign both Dawson
and Raines—not likely, but possible—they might be
willing to part with Tim Wallach, a third baseman
who would wear well on either side of Chicago. He
not only keeps the ball from getting to the outfield
but can hit it that far, too. If they can imagine such
a rarity in their midst, the Cubs and the White Sox
should shadow him, at all costs.

Usually, teams that finish on the brink of first
place will tend to stay reasonably pat. But there
were no division races this season and, therefore,
no excuse for false hopes or inactivity. Besides,
though owners will cry poor, it was a very good
year. All teams exceeded 1 million in attendance,
and the post-season fallout was exceptionally healthy
for the sport. The playoff and World Series games
weren't always textbook stuff, but they meant magnificent entertainment.

Much as this space would cherish more day
games, there is no sound argument for it. Seven
night games in the World Series produced boffo
ratings. More fans watched; more people who might
become fans watched. The notion that we will pro-
duce an entire generation of youths who never saw
a World Series game doesn't wash, not when 8 of
every 10 TV sets in New York is tuned to baseball
on a Sunday morning. And if players don't like late
starts and late finishes, they should remember that
their demands have created need for greater reve-

nue. It's not the networks running the game; it's the banks.

As for the World Series outcome, Chicagoans need extend no sympathy whatsoever to the bereaved fans of Boston. Only two teams have waited longer than 68 years to win it all, and both of those teams sleep here. Besides, the Red Sox should still suffer for trading away Babe Ruth. What might the Cubs or the White Sox have done if they had owned him? Don't answer that. You're not supposed to get aggravated again until April.

But let this chapter end on a more positive note with Bill Moor's predictions, written right before the 1987 season opener.

WILL 1987 TURN INTO CUBS' YEAR? WELL, LET'S SEE . . .
by Bill Moor

It is a time for quiet optimism if you are a Chicago Cub fan.

"Rooting for the Cubs in 1987, will be like going straight to heaven." (As cruel as it may seem, sports writers generally get paid better than poets.)

I didn't make White Sox predictions this time because all 17 Sox fans in town said I knew absolutely nothing about their team. I had to agree after only being able to name two Sox stars—Carlton Fisk and Herbert Baines.

It is a different story with the Cubs. The following story is a little different, too.

APRIL

Cub catcher Jody Davis tried to talk management into letting two other Davises—Sammy and Ron—switch places on Opening Day. "I think we would be better off with Ron Davis singing the national anthem and Sammy Davis Jr. in the bullpen than vice versa," grumbled the catcher, who already has seen too much of Ron Davis' $700,000 arm.

. . . Jody Davis is not the only Cub catcher with gripes during the first month. Manager Gene Michael gets the names of backup catcher Jim Sundberg and Ryne Sandberg mixed up on the lineup card on two different occasions and second baseman Sandberg has to take the first pitch behind the plate. "I'm the one with the mustache," says Sandberg, as 50 more female fans swoon.

. . . All four of Andre Dawson's homers during the month are against Montreal—his old team. Rick Sutcliffe wins his first three starts.

At month's end: Cubs 12–8, two games behind Cards and tied with Mets.

MAY

Keith Moreland keeps his batting average above .330 but has some problems at third base. "He must be missing right field because he's throwing enough balls out here," said Dawson who has learned to play the carom off the first-base wall quite well.

. . . President Ronald Reagan, an old Cub announcer, agrees to pull his stint in the broadcast booth for the recovering Harry Caray and is penciled in for the May 4th game against the Giants. However, he somehow ends up at Comiskey Park and announces the White Sox–Yankees game instead. "When did the Cubs put in lights," he asks.

... Leon Durham hits for the cycle against Atlanta and Scott Sanderson goes on the disabled list
again.

At month's end: Cubs 28–20, 3½ games behind
Cards and 1½ behind the Mets.

JUNE

After the Cubs lose seven of eight at Wrigley—
including four games against Pittsburgh—Jim Frey
comes out of the broadcast booth to take over for
Michael. Meanwhile, Cub president Dallas Green
sends Michael up to the broadcast booth and then
tells him to jump.

... Moreland and Shawon Dunston are on a
record-setting pace for most errors by the left side
of an infield. Box seats behind first base are no
longer such a hot item.

... Both Moreland and Dunston stay hot at the
plate but not hot enough for their batting averages
to be quite as high as their fielding averages. Dunston is moved to leadoff.

At month's end: Cubs 41–36, seven games behind
Cards, 4½ behind Mets and one behind the surprising Pirates.

JULY

After the Cubs cut the number of beer vendors
by 50 percent at the beginning of the season, they
now do the same with custodial workers. "There's
not as much work to do since the cutback on beer
sales," said Green. "The johns aren't always over-
flowing like they used to."

... The only place beer can be found in Wrigley
during the eighth and ninth innings is in the Cub
clubhouse. Unfortunately, that's when everyone else
is wishing for a drink with the middle relief "team"

of Dickie Noles, Frank DiPino and Ron Davis owning a combined 6.37 ERA.

   . . . Cub leaders: Moreland .327, Dawson 21 homers and 67 RBIs, Sandberg 37 stolen bases, Sutcliffe 12–5, Lee Smith 21 (of the Cubs' 23) saves.

   At month's end: Cubs 55–47, six games behind
Cards and five behind the Mets.

AUGUST

With Dawson, Bob Dernier and Brian Dayett playing quite well together in the outfield, the Bleacher
Bums label them "the 3-Ds" and wear the cardboard
movie glasses from the '50s. "I'm just glad we're per-
forming in the matinee," said Dawson, relishing 81
games of daytime baseball in Wrigley Field.

   . . . When Cub coach John Vukovich leaves to become the Phillies manager, Green names Jimmy Piersall as a full-time coach. The only stipulation: Piersall must walk backwards anytime he is in Wrigley
Field. Green says it has nothing to do with the fact
that Piersall had run around the bases backwards
after Green had served up Piersall's 100th career
homer. "Somebody needs to cover our rear," says
Green. "That's all it is."

   . . . Sandberg, batting .322 and making only one
error in the field, appears to be putting together an
MVP year once again. Steve Trout matches Sutcliffe
with his 14th victory.

   At month's end: Cubs 72–59, three games behind
Cards and 1½ behind the slumping Mets.

SEPTEMBER

Frey has the Cubs gaining on the Cardinals and
when Sandberg blasts his 20th home run, he joins
Dawson, Moreland, Durham and Davis over that
mark. The Cub lineup is labeled the "Frey swatters"
as the competition starts dropping like flies.

... The Cubs sweep the Cardinals in Busch Stadium to take the National League East lead for the first time in the season.

... Dunston and Moreland go 17 straight games without either of them making an error. "It's helped since the bruises on my chest have healed," Moreland admits.

... Jamie Moyer pitches a no-hitter against St. Louis on Aug. 27 without getting a strikeout.

... The Cubs clinch three days later in Pittsburgh on Sutcliffe's 20th victory. He lives up to his springtime offer and puts $100,000 in Dawson's pocket. Dawson returns it and holds out for $200,000.

At month's end: Cubs 92–66, five games ahead of Cards with four games to go in October.

OCTOBER

The Cubs beat the Reds, 4–2, in the National League playoffs to win their first pennant in 42 years.

They then pound the Yankees, 4–1, in the World Series for their first Series championship since 1908.

Dutch Reagan announces that final game and then announces he is running for a third term. "No, Mr. President, you get three strikes in baseball, but only two chances as President."

Cub fans aren't listening. They are busy celebrating under the stars—in Busch Stadium.[5]

– 8 –

CUB LEGEND
AND LORE

What follows are some of the interesting comments and stories I came across in doing research for this book. **For example, more than 100 years ago, A.G. Spalding wrote of the problems of owning and running a baseball team in terms that P.K. Wrigley, his son William and countless general managers would find right on the mark:**

A few years ago I happened to be paying a business visit to a city of some importance in the Middle West. The owner of the local club, whom I had known in former years, learning of my presence, sent a complimentary invitation to attend a series of ball games then scheduled for that city. I went, and from the grandstand sent my card to the magnate who was on the bench below, pencil and card in hand, industriously keeping score and directing his players in the game. He responded at once by coming to my side.

I was not prepared for the change I noted in my friend's appearance. He had been a ball player in other days, a fellow of fine physique, active and strong. Now he was attenuated; his hand trembled as he marked the score card; deep furrows crossed his forehead; his once dark hair had turned to gray; he was prematurely an old man. The game progressed, and favorably for his team. When it was ended he said: "Thank God, we've won. We needed that game very badly." Then he added: "Spalding, do you know that I'm a miserable, mental and physical wreck? I can't stand the strain much longer. My wife, too, is disgusted with the whole business. I've made some money, and we're going to buy a farm and get out of Base Ball." It was a simple story, but it portrayed the experiences of many another.

The responsibilities of a Base Ball club owner are great and his trials are many. While those who are ignorant of the troubles that beset his path regard him with envy, he is an ever-present "buffer," receiving the oft-repeated blows of opposing interests. He must stand between the public and its relentless demands for impossibilities. He must provide grounds easily accessible, and fit them up with elaborate grandstand, bleachers, club house and toilets, that shall meet all requirements of comfort, cleanliness and convenience. His grounds must be located as close by many avenues of rapid transit as possible. He must make sacrifice of much money to save time for patrons who want to come late to games in great throngs and depart early in a solid body. If the trolley lines provide inadequate facilities for handling the crowds, the magnate is to blame!

He must stand between the press and the interests of his club in many ways. At least twice a day must he receive representatives of evening and morning papers, and by "soft words" turn away the "wrath" of adverse criticism that is always seeking to discover something with which to find fault. He must be ready to answer diplomatically, satisfactorily and promptly any impudent question that may come from the lips of an irresponsible reporter. "Why don't you release Murphy?" "What do you play O'Brien on second for?" "Why don't you strengthen your pitching staff?" "Say, are you going to sell Corrigan?" These are a few samples of conundrums that come to the club owner, and which he must adroitly answer, skillfully parry, or invoke the ire of the interrogator, with its inevitable results.

He must stand by his team, good, bad or indifferent. He must receive the brunt of hostile comment directed against his players, whether merited or not, from both press and patrons, apologizing for shortcomings where they exist, excusing as accidental errors in play that cost him infinitely more than they could possibly cost anyone else on earth.

He must hear and patiently consider the never-ending stream of complaints growing out of jealousies and ambitions among his players, and must, for the sake of the game, and in his own personal interests, maintain the *esprit de corps* of all members of the team. He must listen to fault finding on the part of the men with the manager he has placed over them, and, acting as judge, must be patient, impartial and just, insisting upon proper deference being paid to the official and at the same time requiring the manager to be fair and reasonable in his treatment of players.

He must be present at as many games as possible, watching the individual work of the team, that he may be personally advised of the capacity of each in order to weed out the weaklings. Meanwhile it is important that he should have his eye on the players of other teams in the league, in the hopes of picking up here and there an artist unappreciated by the manager under whom he is playing. He must be on the grounds to see that order and decorum are preserved, and on occasion he must stand between the umpire and the mob.

Again, he must be big enough to rise above the petty annoyances that thrust themselves upon him. Put yourself in the magnate's place a moment for illustration of this point. All the afternoon you have sat watching the game. It has been characterized by many embarrassing incidents. It has been an "off day" for your team. The boys have made too many errors, and the visitors have been on their mettle. Every close decision has seemed to be against you. The game has ended with a score showing your nine to have the small figures. Everything has gone wrong. The attendance has been light. The crowd is glowering in disgust. You turn from the grounds, thinking to escape to your home, where you may forget the Base Ball business and its discouragements for just a little while. But, alas! Every man you meet is loaded with the same question. "What was the score today?" You are perfectly aware that your interrogator knows the score as well as you do. You saw him in the grandstand, where he caught your eye half a dozen times just as errors had been scored against your team. But you must feign a cheerfulness you do not feel and make a civil answer. Then you must control the ire arising within you as he asks: "What in the d—l is the matter with *your* club, anyhow?" "Can't *your* boys play the game any more?" "Where on earth did *you* get the lobster *you* are playing on third?" Remarks similar to these come from every man you meet on the homeward path. And next day, when the game has been brilliantly won by your team, the bombardment of exclamations and interrogatories is hardly more satisfactory, for now the jubilant fan, in the exuberance of his joy, shouts to the ears of all the world, "How was that?" "What's the matter with *our* boys?" "Say, it looks as if *we'd* got the flag cinched for sure this year, don't it?" And so forth and so on. *Your* club in defeat, with anathemas on the side for *you*. *Our* team in victory, with the bouquets for *us*.

And at night when, harrassed and worried by the embarrassments and perplexities of the day, the magnate seeks needed rest, thoughts of other trials, troubles and tribulations force themselves upon his mind, driving sleep from his tired eyelids. And, if perchance sweet sleep shall come to restore in part his wasted energies, that ever-ready instrument of torture, the telephone, is used by the ubiquitous reporter to call him and ask him for the line-up of to-morrow's game.

And in addition to these are those who fill the ranks of magnates still living, but who have either been forced to leave active Base Ball management in order to escape nervous collapse, or who are yet in the field, carrying on the work, but all the time conscious that they must soon retire—or join the silent majority.

I met James A. Hart, late President of the Chicago Base Ball Club, of the National League, one day after he had sold his interest to its present owner. He had retired, broken in health and completely discouraged. He had greatly improved when I met him, and I said: "Well, James, you're looking fine. Don't you regret having got out of the game?" "Not a regret," answered he. "I'm getting all right again, and life is going to be worth living once more; but it wouldn't be with a ball club on my hands."[1]

Johnny Evers had some observations about managing and baseball players that sound like they were written yesterday:

The position of manager of a team in a major league is one of the most nerve racking, exhausting and desperate in the calendar of work. Primarily, the manager is responsible for the creating and assembling of the team,

The Cubs—first in the heart of America.
(Illustration by Susan Woznicki)

in which duty there are hundreds of opportunities to make mistakes. He is responsible for the condition of the men, both in preparation for the season and during the entire playing season. He is responsible for the selection of the pitchers every day; in this alone a bad manager could cause a team to drop from first to last place in a month. Upon him rests the burden of deciding what style of attack and defense shall be used in any game or in the crises of the game. More than that, he is held responsible by the spectators and by the press, which is severe, and by the "fans," who add cruelty to criticism, for every defeat.

Ishmael would have felt as if he was the guest of honor compared to the manager who with a strong "paper" team finishes far down in the race, and Lazarus and Job could not have felt as sore and boiling as he. In addition, the manager frequently must either endure or suppress criticism and open opposition in his own ranks. The day Job's biggest boil broke he must have felt exactly as did Tom Burns one afternoon when he was managing the Chicago club.

"Push it off to right field," he ordered the batter who was starting to the plate.

"Why, you old gray-headed stiff, you hit .212 the last season you played," responded the player.

The crowd which cheers the players has little conception of the trials and tribulations of the manager who, perhaps, crouches unseen and forgotten (by the crowd) in the corner of the bench. The public does not realize that he is dealing with twenty-two ultra-independent athletes, vulgarly healthy, frankly outspoken and unawed by any authority or pomp. Only persons who have one child, which possesses four grandparents, and twenty or thirty aunts all trying to spoil it, can understand in full the difficulties of the manager's job.

Ball players are about as spoiled, unreasonable and pampered as a matinee idol, and are worse because they are usually young and have not even the saving grace of experience to guide them. The average major league player is a youth who has jumped from small wages to a comfortable income in a few weeks, from the criticism of the home crowd of a few dozen persons to the applause and cheers of perhaps twenty thousand persons. He is sought after, flattered and pampered. He meets men and women of high standing who thoughtlessly praise him. The surprising thing is that ball players who succeed are not worse spoiled.

The young ball player has a brilliant day; he is exalted. He has a bad day, and the excited abuse heaped upon him by the crowd burns his sensitive soul. He becomes cynical and bitter. In a short time he either is a "bug" or a "grouch." He has all the day, except a short time in the afternoon and perhaps an hour in the morning, to exult over his triumphs or mourn over his errors and in his bitterness he loses faith both in friends and enemies.

That stage requires several years to wear away. In about five seasons the player realizes that the public is fickle, that it does not mean its applause any more than it means its abuse. He begins to understand that in its excitement the crowd is "cussing the cards, not the players." Then he generally grows more philosophical. This does not always happen, however. There was one player who, after years of playing, was going to desert the Chicago team because one night he was assigned to lower berth number five instead of to number seven.

It is small wonder that the major league players become spoiled. The hotel arrangements all are made for them; their baggage is checked, the train connections, berths, and carriages are all arranged for by the manager or secretary. The player is told when to go, where to

go, and how to go and some players after years of traveling are almost as helpless as if they never had been
on a train. On many occasions when a player wants to
make a journey by himself the manager is compelled to
purchase his tickets, find his train, and send him to it
in a carriage. There was a player with the St. Louis club
a few years ago who asked permission of the manager
to lay over on Sunday at Cincinnati en route from Boston to Philadelphia.

The trials of a manager with twenty men, the majority of them grown children, under his charge, who is
forced to soothe their injured feelings, condole with them
in their troubles, cheer them in their blues and check
them in their exuberance, may better be imagined than
told.

One evening after Frank Chance had won two World's
Championships, he sat gloomily silent for a long time.
The big, hearty, joyous boy who had come from California a dozen years before was battered, grizzled, care-
worn and weary. Still young, his fine face showed lines
of care and worry and a few gray hairs streaked his head.
He was thirty-two and looked old. For a long time he sat
musing. Then he looked up and smiled grimly.

"This business is making a crab out of me," he remarked.[2]

**Johnny Evers recalled a prank, a pick-off play and
a cagey pitcher in stories too good to remain forgotten.**

The prank:
    One spring a cold rain fell upon the Chicago Cubs
training camp, and continued to fall incessantly,
dismally putting an end to practice just as the players were working off the first soreness.

The dejected athletes, knowing they would have to undergo the soreness and stiffness all over again, moped in the hotel. Toward the middle of the gloomy, cold afternoon some one proposed to turn a bath room into a Turkish bath establishment. The steam was turned on, cracks stuffed and the hot water was allowed to pour into the tub until the room was superheated and filled with steam. Four husky players, in Adamic condition, proceeded to swath themselves in blankets and take off weight. Half a dozen bath towels, folded, were placed on the steam radiator, and the players took turns sitting on the radiator with half a dozen blankets wrapped around them. Chance's turn came. He adjusted the blankets, parted them carefully, and sat down. Steinfeldt had a narrow escape from being killed, and Chance to this day thinks it was Steinfeldt who took the towels off the radiator.[3]

The pick-off play:

Tinker and Evers plotted a play a few years ago that caught many men and furnished the spectators much joy. When a hit-and-run play is attempted and the batter hits a fly to the outfield, the base runner hearing the crack of the bat, must judge from actions of the fielders in front of him what has happened. When such a situation came up Tinker and Evers went through all the motions of trying to stop a grounder, or diving after a hit. The runner would fear being forced out at second and tear along under the impression the ball had gone through the infield. Sometimes he would be nearly to third base before the outfielder, catching the ball, would toss it to the first baseman and complete the double play.

Sherwood Magee was caught three times in one season on the play, and finally in Philadelphia, the Cubs
tried it again. Magee, not to be caught again, gave
them the laugh and jogged back to first, whereupon
Schulte dropped the ball, threw it to second, and
Tinker fired it back to first, completing the double
play.[4]

The cagey pitcher:

Players of the present day are prone to scoff at
the tales of the prowess of "Matty" Kilroy, better
known as "Bazzazaz," a left-handed pitcher who
performed marvels. Most modern pitchers declare
that under present conditions Kilroy would have
been a failure. The little left-hander, after years of
triumph, retired because his arm was hopelessly
worn out. In spite of that fact Tom Burns, when he
assumed charge of the Chicago Club in 1898, resurrected Kilroy, whose arm was so weak, according
to his own admission, he "couldn't break a pane of
glass at fifty feet."

Yet for one season and part of another he pitched
against the strongest clubs and beat them regularly.

Kilroy's success was due almost entirely to his
"Bazzazaz" balk, which he evolved by persistent training. He was the only pitcher who ever balked without balking—if such a thing is possible. In the first
four innings of the first game he pitched against
Baltimore after Burns resurrected him, nine men
reached first base. He caught six of them off the
base and, although two umpires watched every move
he made, they declared that under the rules he did
not balk.

Kilroy explained after his permanent retirement,

his system of training by which he acquired the "bazzazaz balk."

"I see the old soup bone was ready for the undertaker," he said. "So I goes to work on the balk. I always had a good balk motion, but wanted a better one. I spent half the winter in the side yard at home with a chalk mark on the wall for first base and another on the fence for the home plate. I practiced morning and afternoon, making from two hundred and fifty to four hundred throws a day with my wrist and forearm trying to hit the first base line while looking at the other one and without moving either my feet or body.

"By practicing I got so I could shoot the ball faster to first base with wrist and forearm than I could pitch it to the plate with a full swing. That's all there was to it. Just look straight at the plate, pull your hands up against your breast, raise your left one to the level of your ear, then drive the ball to first without looking until after it starts, and you've got him. The umpire can't see whether you look before you throw or not."

He did get them. Probably he made twenty thousand practice throws at the chalk mark, but he perfected the motion that enabled him to pitch two years after his arm was "dead."[5]

And it is thanks to Evers that we know the origin of the one-handed catch by outfielders. Naturally, it was invented by a Cub:

There is one more interesting incident that stands unique, and it is one by which Jimmy Slagle staved off disaster to the Chicago team in a twenty-inning

battle between Chicago and Philadelphia, which
Reulbach finally won two to one. In the eighteenth
inning of that struggle, with a runner on first base,
Sherwood Magee drove a hard line hit to left center.
Slagle had just shoved his hand into his hip pocket
to get his chewing tobacco when the ball was hit,
and as he started in pursuit of it, he discovered to
his horror that his right hand was caught in the
pocket and refused to come out. A quick jerk failed
to release the hand, and Slagle, racing on, leaped,
stuck up his left hand, and caught the ball, saving
the Cubs. Then he pulled out his tobacco, bit off a
piece, and grinned as the crowd applauded.[6]

The Cubs were also the only team on record to have
a hitter who didn't know which way to run. He was a
31-year-old pitcher in 1902 and his name was Jim St.
Vrain. Jim wasn't a great pitcher. In his sole season in
the majors he lost six of 10 decisions. But he was even
a worse hitter. Although he threw left-handed, he was a
right-handed batter and normally he didn't make contact with the ball.

One day when he returned to the dugout after fan-
ning, manager Frank Selee asked him why he didn't bat
left-handed. St. Vrain said he just never had. The next
time up he decided to try. Swinging at the first pitch he
hit a grounder to Pirate shortstop Honus Wagner. St.
Vrain took off at full speed toward third base!

Wagner fielded the ball and was ready to throw when
he saw the runner heading toward third. He almost threw
there but then remembered that no matter what St. Vrain
was doing, the play was at first.

People kidded St. Vrain, but he was on a roll. He had
amassed three hits in 31 trips when the season ended.
That's three more than most of us got in the major leagues.

It was a Chicago freelance writer named Ron Berler who first made public what has been called "the ex-Cub factor." Noting in 1981 that Montreal could not hope to beat the Dodgers in the playoffs because the Expos had four ex-Cubs on their roster, Berler claimed that it is impossible to win a championship with three or more ex-Cubs on a team. Writes Berler: "Behind every major failure in baseball stands a Chicago Cub. It's no secret that the Cubs have always been 'different' from other major leaguers. In fact, some say that the Cubs are the Moonies of baseball, that the club possesses eerie, bewitching powers over its players."

Jim Brosnan, an ex-Cub pitcher, claims that he had to go through psychoanalysis to deal with his "Cubness."

Berler's theory has only one exception when applied all the way back to 1945. In 1960, the Pirates beat the Yankees despite having three ex-Cubs—Burgess, Baker and Hoak—on the team. Brosnan explained that the exception only proved the rule:

"Hoak played for the Brooklyn Dodgers, a very good team, before he was traded to the Cubs, a very bad team. As far as Hoak was concerned, he went right from Brooklyn to Pittsburgh without ever stopping in Chicago. He refused to accept the fact that he was a Cub. He had nothing but obscene words for the Cubs and their organization; he even hated P.K. Wrigley." "Hoak," Brosnan concluded, "is quite possibly the only man who ever conquered his Cubness."

Another part of Cub legend has to do with goats. During the 20 or so years that the Cubs trained on Catalina Island, Cub players frequently ran into goats while doing road work in the mountains. It is not recorded who won those encounters. In 1945 the goat came to Clark

HIGHEST PAIN THRESHOLD I'VE EVER
SEEN .. PROBABLY A CUBS FAN...

(Illustration by Ben Templeton and Tom Forman)

and Addison. William G. Sianis, known as "Billy Goat," brought his pet goat to the World Series. Although he had box seat tickets, it was explained to him that the Cubs did not want to offend their other customers with the smell of a goat in their midst. Before leaving the park, "Billy Goat" slapped a hex on the Cubs. When they proceeded to lose the Series to the Tigers, Sianis is said to have sent a telegram to Mr. Wrigley saying simply, "Now who stinks?"

Sam Sianis, "Billy Goat's" nephew, brought Billy Goat XX, a descendent of the '45 goat, to Wrigley Field on opening day in 1984. He was welcomed this time and the goat hexed the opposition, helping the Cubs win. Asked how it happens, Sianis replied, "I don't know. But the goat knows."

In 1982, Bob Verdi wrote a classic column that is well worth repeating:

HERE'S AN UPBEAT CUB RECORD
by Bob Verdi

In more ways than one, the Cubs are changing their tune.

For the worse part of four decades, their unrequited lovers have sworn on stacks of tear-stained ticket stubs that it wouldn't take much to make a musical comedy about this team. If a composer could supply the music, the Cubs easily could provide the comedy.

However, comma, as part of their new tradition, the Cubs have solicited one Terry Cashman to enhance their image. Cashman, a major-league baseball fan who also enjoys watching the Cubs, has released a song that captures the history of the franchise. Even so, the beat is strictly up.

The title of the melody is, simply, "Baseball and The Cubs." Feel free to purchase a copy and enjoy it. Probably, it will be the Cubs' only record of the season.

Cashman, of course, is not breaking in with the Cubs. He doesn't qualify because he's not from Philadelphia. However, he's the same fellow who, last spring, cut "Willie, Mickey and The Duke," a delightful disc that caught on with the American public a lot easier than Joe Strain caught onto second base.

Cashman's list of credits in the music business is impressive. For several years, he was a producer for the late Jim Croce. Before that, Cashman wrote "Sunday Will Never Be The Same," which was made popular by, you should pardon the expression, Spanky and Our Gang. Cashman, in fact, is so big that he even has appeared on American Bandstand with Dick Clark, the eternal teenager.

Anyway, Terry Cashman is perfect for Wrigley Field, and that's where he'll be Saturday, singing his new song before the Cubs' exhibition game against the White Sox. Listen carefully. It may be the last Cub score for a while that won't make you cry.

"I'm very excited about it," Cashman said Thursday. "I've never been to Wrigley Field, but I hear it's a great park."

Cashman grew up in New York, not far from the Polo Grounds. At one time, he was courted by the Detroit Tigers, who gave him a bonus for signing and sent him to Montgomery, Ala. Cashman's minor-league career was fleeting. As a pitcher, the Tigers discovered, he made a better hummer. He changed his career motives, and he also changed his name, from Dennis Minogue to Terry Cashman.

But his devotion to baseball never changed. While Minogue-Cashman was still a kid, one of the burning questions in the Big Apple was which team had the best center fielder? Was it Willie Mays of the Giants, Mickey Mantle of the Yankees or Duke Snider of the Dodgers? Admittedly, this dilemma lacked the cosmic impact of the game as played in Wrigley Field, where customers merely fretted about whether Frank Ernaga or Ed Winceniak were fast enough to chase down some of the rockets to which Vito Valentinetti gave rise.

Be that as it may, Cashman became hooked on the sport. One day not long ago, a friend gave Cashman a rare picture of Willie, Mickey and The Duke walking in from center field at an Old Timers' Game in New York. They were facing the crowd, their famous numbers emblazoned on the backs of their jerseys, their physiques altered slightly, but not their stature. The nostalgia of it all grabbed Terry Cashman by the guitar strings.

"I said to myself that there had to be a song there somewhere," he recalled. "It took me about 20 minutes to put it together. And when I was done with it, I cried."

All the way to the bank, Terry Cashman cried. For much of last summer, while he was talkin' baseball, there was no baseball because the owners called a strike. Cashman's creation was played over and over by the nation's radio and TV outlets, providing an idyllic interlude to the financial wrangling of the day. "Willie, Mickey and The Duke" recognizes the sport as a sport. There is nary a mention of the free-agent draft, renegotiating contracts or Ray Grebey. Unlike Bowie Kuhn, Terry Cashman had acted in the best interests of baseball.

"It got a tremendous reaction," said Cashman. "Unlike a lot of songs for fans, though, it was not a 'Rah Rah Fernando!' type thing. It was more sentimental, more emotional, than a song about one player who was hot at the time, or something like that. I didn't want it to sound hokey. I was surprised how well it was received. It made me realize more than ever the hold that baseball has over our country.

"The only complaint I got, even though I mentioned a lot of players from a lot of teams and eras, was that people thought it was a New York song. Because of Willie, Mickey and The Duke, I suppose. A guy from Detroit said he liked it, but he also said, 'Where's Al Kaline?' That's how it grew into this."

At present, Cashman says 18 major league teams have asked him to take the same tune, the same tone, and use it with player names from each franchise's legacy. For most clubs, that would be no problem. The heritage is rich. But the Cubs aren't like most clubs.

How do you devote an aria to them without an unfortunate chorus about Herman Franks using his jersey as a napkin for his Skoal drippings, or without an embarrassing verse about Larry Biittner losing a fly ball beneath his hat?

"It was easy," insisted Cashman. "They've had some great names and great moments in their past."

True to his words, Cashman has written rhyme about the Cubs, even when there is no reason. He sings of Jolly Cholly, Gabby, Ernie, Hank, Cavarretta, Tinker, Evers, Chance, Kessinger, Beckert, Hack Wilson, Stan Hack, The Vulture, Handsome Ransom and many, many more. Cashman even brought his opera up to date by including Lee Elia, Dallas Green, Bill Buckner, Larry Bowa, Tye, Campbell, Keith, Davis, Durham and all that gang.

For all the toasts, there are no roasts. Cashman doesn't mention the Cubs' fainting spell of 1969, the starting rotation of 1982, the College of Coaches, Ernie Broglio, Bill Wrigley's extravagance, Dave Kingman's boat, Bob Kennedy's wit or The Marshall Plan.

"I didn't get the name of my favorite Cub in there, either," regretted Cashman. "Turk Lown."

But a lot of other luminaries have been omitted. Where have you gone Marcelino Solis, Elvin Tappe, Harry Chiti, Merritt Ranew, Garry Jestadt, Norm Gigon, Mel Roach, Phil Gagliano and Manny Jimenez? Perhaps they are names to be played later.

"I'm excited," repeated Cashman. "I hope the people will like it. It'll be available on 45."

Ah, that was a very good year for the Cubs. Their last very good one, in fact. Terry Cashman has been nice to the Cubs. When writing a song about their accomplishments, after all, he could have used another title. Silent Night.

An expert on Cub fans, Phoebe Medow of Way to Go travel agency in Chicago, the major organizer of Cub fan tours over the years, makes it clear that you can take the Cub fan out of Chicago but you can't . . .

During the slow years of the Cubs' recent history, we took about 50 people to Cincinnati and continued on to Atlanta. I missed the Cincinnati days because I was away on another trip, and a couple of people from the Way to Go office accompanied the group. I arrived to meet them in Atlanta and was down in front (the Braves give us great seats) for the game. We were seated directly behind the Cubs' dugout; in effect, right on top of it.

Five members of our group, who habitually spent their afternoons in the Wrigley Field bleachers, began chanting into the dugout, "FRANKS MUST GO!" "FRANKS MUST GO!" "FRANKS MUST GO!" There's not too much excitement in that park (between innings the public address system announces prizes of bags of onions and insecticide spray "to make your life a little less rotten") and somehow the camera crew decided to find the source of the shouting. The five Chicagoans, wearing their Cub paraphernalia, were enshrined on the giant TV screen over center field, in full color, larger than life . . . screaming for the ejection of their team manager. A couple of ladies from my group went to sit at the top of the seating area for the duration of the game (they never did speak to me ever again).

When we returned to the hotel, some of our group were already in the lobby, having gone out of the ball park for their own reasons. The first words I heard were, "You're on television and the announcers are laughing that the Chicago fans are booing their own team." It was not our most glorious moment.

More recently in Atlanta, Ron Cey, better known in the baseball world as "The Penguin," was up to bat for the Cubs. In back of me an Atlanta fan shouted at Ron, "Stand up. We can't see you." "Stand up, Cey—we can't see you." Unexpectedly, Cey hit a towering home run that is still travelling. As he walked back into the dugout after touring the base path, I asked quietly, "Can you see him now?" Even the heckler laughed.[7]

The Cubs and their fans! **Listen to Charlie Grimm:**

I know this much in baseball—you can't win 'em all. And this includes that sideline business with the fans.

For years I had a special fan in Wrigley Field. He always was in the same seat behind our third base dugout. He would mellow in the later innings after a few beers. He's keep up a running, friendly conversation while I coached at third base.

"Nice going, Grimm!" he'd shout. "You're doing all right. You'll always do all right. I'm for you 100 percent."

On this particular day, it rained all morning. Finally the sun came out, but the infield was mushy in spots. We were playing the Pirates and came into the ninth inning with the score tied. Bill Jurges was on second base when Woody English hit a line drive single to right field. Paul Waner fielded the ball and I gave Jurges the go sign as he came toward me. But he slipped on the grass and landed right near me in the coaching box. I had to hold him up because Waner had fired the ball to the plate. We didn't score that inning. Fact is, we lost in the eleventh.

From the ninth to the sad finish, my erstwhile No. 1 booster berated me. When it was over, he yelled, "Grimm, I'll never come to this park again!

(Illustration by John Trever)

Since the 1908 Cubs World Championship ...
- The U.S. has fought in four wars
- There have been 14 presidents
- U.S. population has increased by 143,000,000
- The Cubs have lost seven World Series
- Halley's Comet has been by twice

I've sat in the same seat for years and have always been for you until now."

What made you change?" I shouted.

"When you start tripping your runners when they come around third base with the winning run, that's the end!" he bellowed.

Well . . . that's what the man thought. And he's paid for the right to say it.[8]

One way or another the Cubs and their fans have gone through life, generation after generation, with happiness and hurts, hope and forgiveness, frustration and humor. All things considered, may it always be so.

NOTES

Chapter 1

1. A.G. Spalding, *America's National Game* (New York: American Sports Publishing Co., 1911), pp. 522–26.
2. Mike Kelly in the *New York Sun*, quoted in Spalding, *op. cit.*, p. 265.
3. Billy Sunday, cited in Spalding, *op. cit.*, pp. 440–41.
4. Cited in Spalding, *op. cit.*, p. 441.
5. Adrian C. Anson, *A Ball Player's Career* (Chicago: Era Publishing Co., 1900), p. 109.
6. *Ibid.*, pp. 123–24.
7. *Ibid.*, pp. 115–16.
8. *Ibid.*, p. 299.
9. *Ibid.*, pp. 302–03.

Chapter 2

1. Johnny Evers, *Touching Second* (Chicago: Reilly and Britton, 1910), pp. 16–17.
2. Cited by Spalding, *op. cit.*, pp. 443–45.
3. Evers, *op. cit.*, p. 92.
4. Cited in G.H. Fleming, *The Unforgettable Season* (New York: Holt, Rinehart and Winston, 1981), pp. 126–27.
5. Evers, *op. cit.*, pp. 247–48.
6. *Ibid.*, p. 94.
7. Cited by Fleming, *op. cit.*, p. 309.
8. Evers, *op. cit.*, pp. 266–67.

9. Warren Brown, *The Chicago Cubs* (New York: G.P. Putnam's Sons, 1946), pp. 64–65.

Chapter 3

1. Warren Brown, *op. cit.*, pp. 94–99, 101–10.
2. Frederick G. Lieb, *Connie Mack* (New York: G.P. Putnam's Sons, 1945), pp. 223–30.

Chapter 4

1. Charlie Grimm, *Grimm's Baseball Tales* (South Bend: Diamond Communications, 1983), pp. 60 ff.
2. *Ibid.*, pp. 103–09.

Chapter 5

1. Edgar Munzel, *The Sporting News*, February 21, 1950.
2. Neil R. Gazel, *Chicago Daily News*, July 14, 1951.
3. Warren Brown, *Chicago Herald-American*, July 27, 1951.
4. Davis J. Walsh, *Chicago Herald-American*, January 21, 1952.
5. Warren Brown, *Chicago Herald-American*, March 30, 1954.
6. Jim Langford, *The Game Is Never Over* (South Bend: Icarus, 1980), pp. 104–06.
7. *Ibid.*, pp. 108–09.
8. Bob Ibach, Chicago Cubs Program Magazine, Volume 5, No. 2, pp. 51–52.

Chapter 6

1. Eddie Gold and Art Ahrens, *The New Era Cubs* (Chicago: Bonus Books, 1985), p. 122.

2. Jim Langford, *The Game Is Never Over* (South Bend: Icarus, 1980), p. 144.

3. Bob Logan, *So You Think You're a Die-Hard Cub Fan* (Chicago: Contemporary, 1985), pp. 99–100.

4. Jack Brickhouse, *Thanks for Listening!* (South Bend: Diamond Communications, 1986), p. 143.

5. Armand Schneider, *New York Post*, July 3, 1976.

Chapter 7

1. Bill Moor, *South Bend Tribune*, September 25, 1984.

2. Bill Moor, *Ibid.*, October 9, 1984.

3. William E. Geist, Esquire, April 1985, pp. 121 ff.

4. Bob Verdi, *Chicago Tribune*, October 31, 1986.

5. Bill Moor, *South Bend Tribune*, April 6, 1987.

Chapter 8

1. A.G. Spalding, *America's National Game* (New York: American Sports Publishing Co., 1911), pp. 425–33.

2. Johnny Evers, *Touching Second* (Chicago: Reilly and Britton, 1910), pp. 76–79.

3. *Ibid.*, pp. 234–35.

4. *Ibid.*, p. 205.

5. *Ibid.*, pp. 229–30.

6. *Ibid.*, p. 299.

7. Phoebe Medow, unpublished manuscript.

8. Charlie Grimm, *Grimm's Baseball Tales* (South Bend: Diamond Communications, 1983), pp. 241–42.